Junkers Ju

in action
Part 1

By Brian Filley

Color By Don Greer

Illustrated By Perry Manley

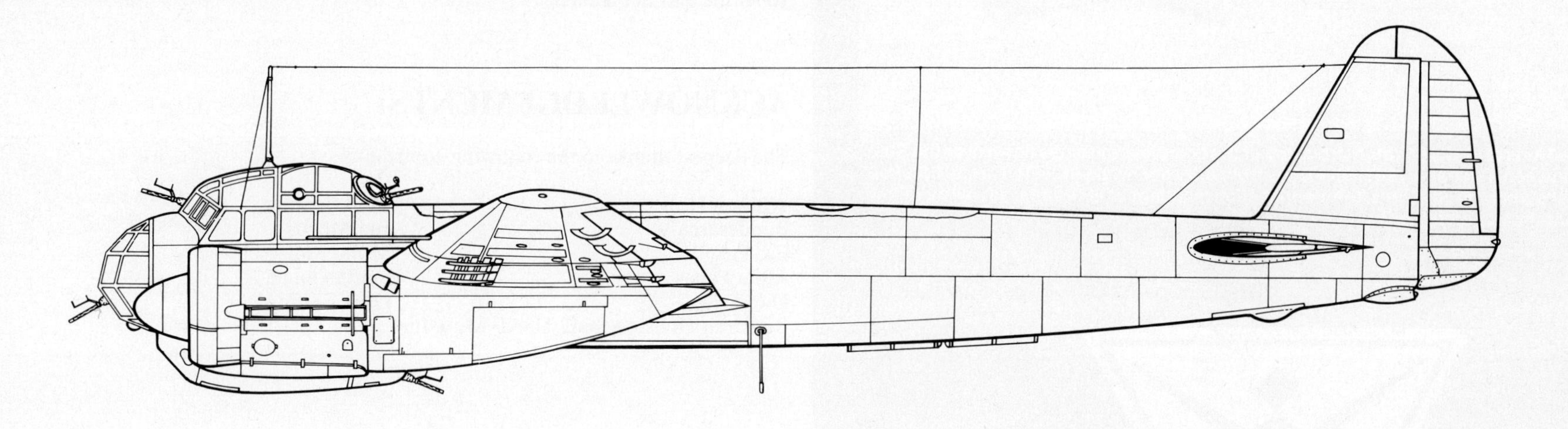

Aircraft Number 85

squadron/signal publications, inc.

A pair of Ju 88A-4s of III/KG 51 return from one of the countless missions flown over the Russian front between 1941 and 1945. 9K+DS is from 8.*Staffel*, while 9K+FR is from 7.*Staffel*. Both have Yellow engine cowl rims, the identification markings of III *Gruppe*, as well as Yellow Eastern Front theater markings.

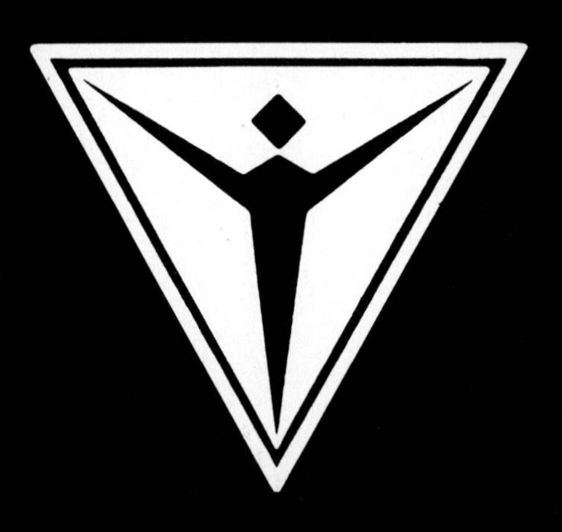

ISBN 0-89747-201-2

If you have any photographs of the aircraft, armor, soldiers or ships of any nation, particularly wartime snapshots, why not share them with us and help make Squadron/Signal's books all the more interesting and complete in the future. Any photograph sent to us will be copied and the original returned. The donor will be fully credited for any photos used. Please send them to:

Squadron/Signal Publications, Inc.
1115 Crowley Drive.
Carrollton, TX 75011-5010.

DEDICATION:

To Annie and her 'kids'.

ACKNOWLEDGEMENTS:

The deepest thanks to the following contributors:

William Hess
Bundesarchiv
E.C.P.A.
Anita Faber
Uwe Feist
Research Division Staff, USAF Museum
Mark Hunter
Jim Mesko
Mihai Moisescu
Smithsonian
Gene Stafford

A Ju 88A-4 of III/LG 1 in flight over the Mediterranean displays the Gothic nose contours typical of the Ju 88 series. The Ju 88A-4 was the most numerous variant of the *Schnell-bomber* produced and was the backbone of the *Luftwaffe* bomber force, serving from the frozen steppes of Russia to the burning deserts of North Africa.

INTRODUCTION

When the Second World War began the *Luftwaffe*, because of the overconfidence of the *Technische Amt* (Technical Office) of the *Reichsluftfahrtministerium* (State Ministry of Aviation or RLM), was dependent on twin-engined medium bombers for offensive operations. *Luftwaffe Kampfgeschwadern* (bomber wings) were equipped with three medium bomber types; the Heinkel He 111, Dornier Do 17, and Junkers Ju 88. Of these, the Junkers Ju 88 had proven itself to be an exceptional aircraft capable of fulfilling a variety of roles. As the war progressed the Ju 88 would be called on to perform as a bomber, day and night fighter, reconnaissance bomber, torpedo bomber, ground attack aircraft, and pilotless bomb; missions never envisioned by its designers.

Development of the Junkers Ju 88 began during 1935 when the *Reichsluftfahrtministerium* (RLM) issued specifications to Junkers, Messerschmitt, Focke-Wulf and Henschel for a three man *Schnell-bomber* (fast bomber). These specifications called for a maximum speed of 310 mph, a bomb load of 1,765 pounds, and defensive armament of one dorsal mounted 7.9MM machine gun with 500 rounds of ammunition. Performance objectives included the ability to clear a sixty-five foot obstacle after a take off run of 765 yards and a rate of climb sufficient to reach 22,965 feet in twenty-five minutes. Equipment specified for the new bomber included a short wave radio, enclosed bomb sight, and provision for high altitude oxygen equipment.

Three firms submitted proposals to meet the RLM specifications,; Messerschmitt, Henschel, and Junkers. The *Technische Amt* considered each proposal, rejecting the Messerschmitt Bf 162/163 and Henschel Hs 127 designs. Junkers had submitted two proposals; a twin-tailed bomber designated the Ju 85 and a cleaner, more conventional design under the designation Ju 88. In the event the Ju 85 was rejected with the Ju 88 being selected for full scale development. The RLM ordered three prototypes under the designations Ju 88V-1, Ju 88V-2 and Ju 88V-3.

Design work on the Ju 88V-1 prototype was initiated by W.H. Evers and Alfred Gassner (an American design consultant) in January of 1936. Construction of the first prototype was started that spring, with the Ju 88V-1 (carrying the civil code D-AQEN), beginning flight trials in late Autumn. The Ju 88V-1 was a low-wing all metal fully cantilever monoplane. The two-spar wings were separate assemblies joined to the fuselage by ball and socket joints. The wings were covered with stressed metal skinning except for the ailerons which were fabric covered.

The prototype was powered by two 1,000 hp Daimler-Benz DB 600Aa 12-cylinder liquid-cooled inline engines housed in long circular cowlings with annular radiators, giving the Ju 88 the appearance of a radial engined aircraft. This appearance was not coincidental, since the Ju 88 had been designed from the outset with the provision that either type of powerplant could be installed. The long engine nacelles contained the rear retracting, electrically-operated twin-oleo main landing gear legs; while the locking, fully castering tail wheel retracted into a well equipped with flush fitting gear doors under the rear fuselage.

The three crewmembers were seated beneath a 'greenhouse' canopy with hinged panels on the top and sides of the canopy. Transparent plexiglass panels were installed on the underside of the pointed semi-solid nose both for use by bombardier and to provide the pilot with a degree of downward view. The bomb load was carried internally on horizontally mounted bomb racks housed in a fuselage bomb bay located between the wing roots.

The Ju 88V-1 prototype's first flight took place on 21 December 1936 with Junkers chief test pilot *Flugkapitän* Kinderman at the controls. The prototype displayed good handling qualities and demonstrated a top speed of approximately 279 mph. Unfortunately the prototype was totally destroyed in an accident after only a few test flights. The test program was interrupted until the Ju 88V-2 (D-AREN) made its first flight on 10 April 1937. The Ju 88V-2 differed from the Ju 88V-1 in that the external radiator air scoops mounted under the engine cowlings were deleted with the cooling system being

The Ju 88V-1 prototype (D-AQEN), which first flew in December of 1936, was destroyed in a crash shortly after beginning its test program. The prototype was painted overall Light Gray with two Yellow fuselage bands, Black codes, and a Red tail banner carrying a Black Swastika on a White circle.

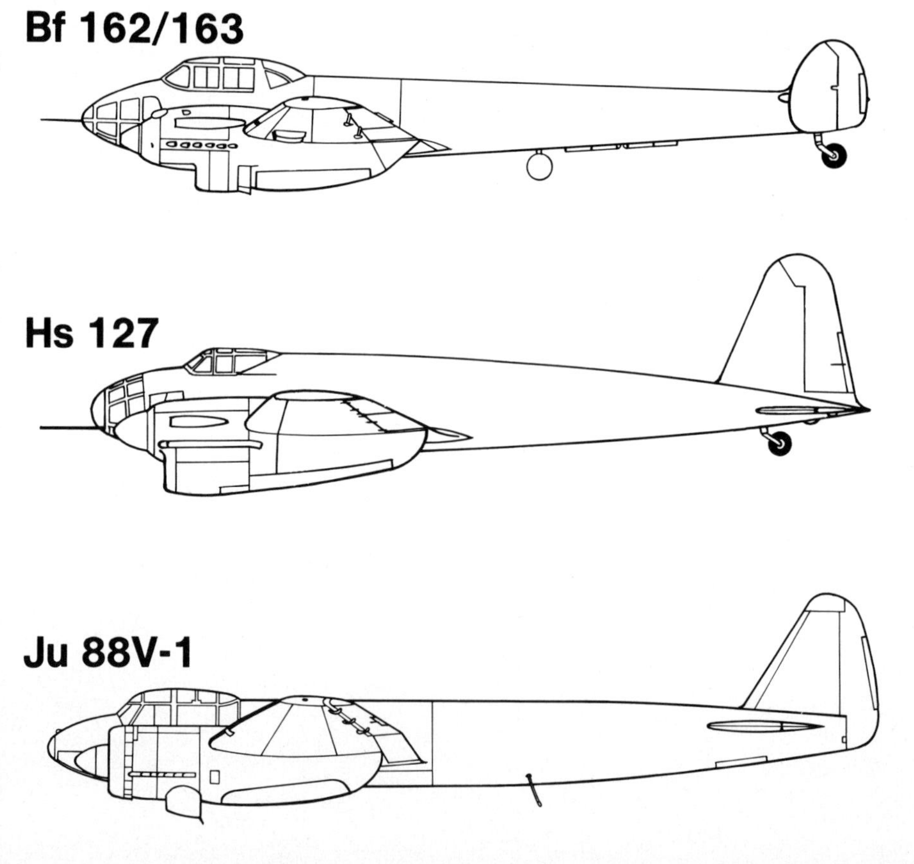

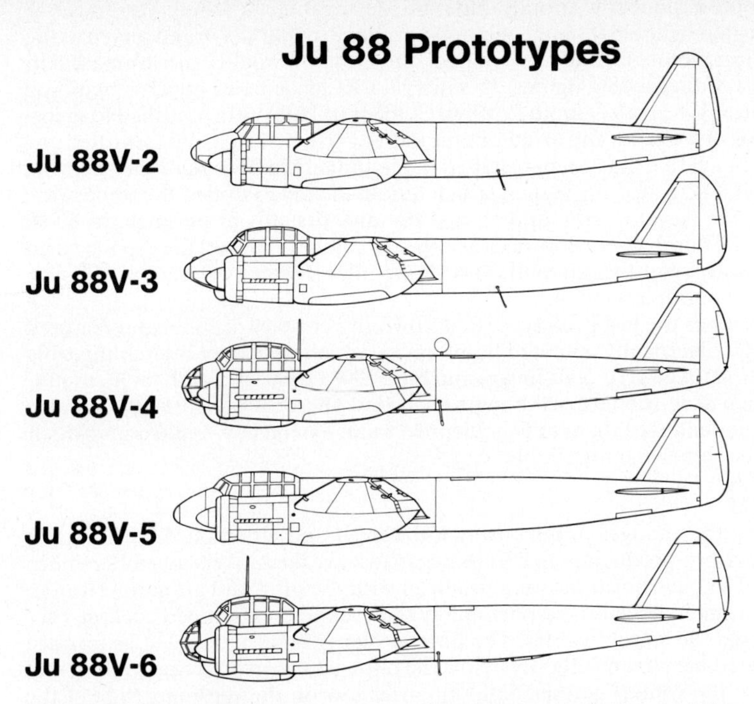

incorporated in slightly enlarged annular radiators at the front of the cowlings. Performance was similar to that of the Ju 88V-1, however, the V-2 was slightly faster, reaching a top speed of 289 mph.

The Ju 88V-3 (D-ASAZ) made its first flight on 13 September 1937 and featured a number of improvements and changes over the second prototype. The 1,000 hp DB 600Aa engines were replaced with 1,100 hp Junkers Jumo 211A engines. To improve lateral stability the rudder area was increased, and the 'greenhouse' canopy was raised to improve crew comfort and visibility. Provision was made for a rear firing 7.9MM machine gun mounted at the rear of the canopy and a fairing was added beneath the starboard side of the nose to house the Lotfe bomb sight periscope. Service evaluations were conducted at the *Erprobungsstelle* (Testing Center) at Rechlin, where the Ju 88V-3 demonstrated a top speed of 323 mph at a gross weight of 18,740 pounds. This performance, along with the favorable endorsements of the test center's pilots, led the RLM to order additional prototypes and requested Junkers to submit plans for full scale dispersed production.

The RLM also requested a number of changes in the next series of prototypes including the capability to serve as a dive bomber, increased defensive armament, and the addition of a fourth crew member. These changes were incorporated into the next prototype, the Ju 88V-4. With the Ju 88V-4, the cockpit was moved forward with the greenhouse canopy again being raised slightly. To improve forward visibility, the semi-solid nose was replaced by a 'beetle's eye' transparent nose section with twenty optically flat plexiglass panels. A ventral 'bathtub' gondola was added beneath the nose offset to the starboard side which covered the belly hatch and provided a housing for both the bombsight and a rear firing 7.9MM MG 15 machine gun. The belly machine gun would be fired by the fourth crewman from a prone position at the rear of the gondola. The rear portion of the 'bathtub' was hinged, opening downward to allow crew access to the interior of the bomber. Later a small pneumatic cylinder was installed on the hatch hinge line to prevent the hatch from dropping open too suddenly. The Ju 88V-4 made its maiden flight on 2 February 1938.

The Ju 88V-5 was modified for attempts on a number of world speed records during the spring of 1939. The 'beetle's eye' nose was replaced with a smooth solid nose cap, a low profile canopy was installed, and paddle bladed propellers with large spinners were added. The twin oleo landing gear was common to the Ju 88V-1 through Ju 88V-5 prototypes.

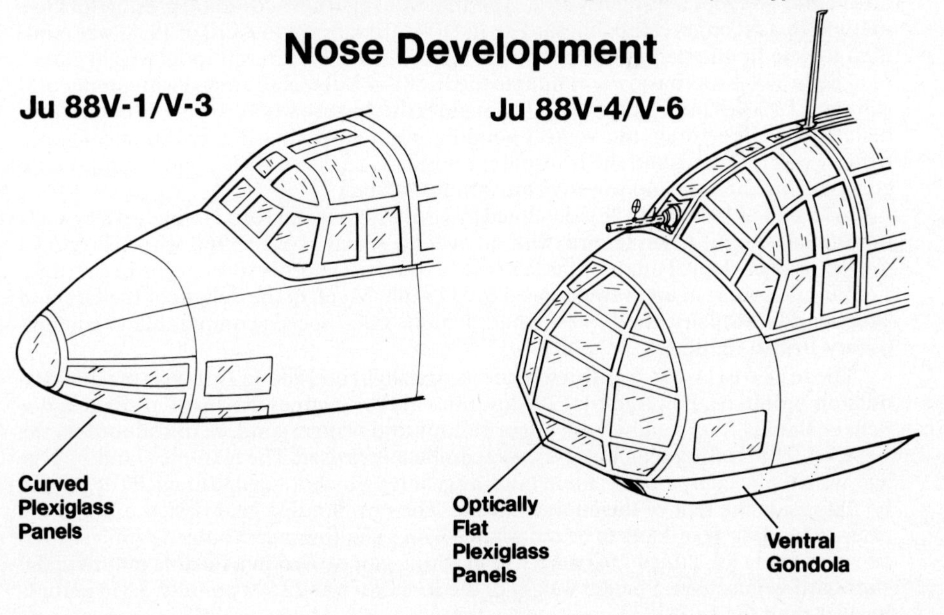

The Ju 88V-6 prototype introduced many of the features found on the initial production Ju 88s. The landing gear was revised with single oleo legs replacing the twin legs of the earlier prototypes. External bomb racks under the wing roots would later be introduced on the Ju 88V-10 prototype for heavier bomb loads.

During this period the German government was intent on gaining as much favorable world publicity for the German aircraft industry as possible. Plans were made to publicly unveil the Ju 88 with a 'publicity prototype' that would garner additional prestige for Germany with a record breaking flight. The Ju 88V-5 (first flown in April of 1938) was modified for use in an attempt on the world's speed record for aircraft in its weight class.

The Ju 88V-5 was basically similar to the Ju 88V-4, but was equipped with production standard 1,200 hp Junkers Jumo 211B-1 engines driving broad chord paddle bladed propellers. To reduce drag, the ventral gondola was removed, a low-profile greenhouse canopy was installed, and the transparent nose was replaced with a pointed solid nose cone leaving the side and lower vision windows intact.

In March of 1939 the Ju 88V-5, piloted by Ernst Siebert and Kurt Heintz, set a new 621 mile closed-circuit speed record, with an average speed of 321.5 mph while carrying a 4,409 pound payload. Four months later the Ju 88V-5 set another speed record, covering a 1242.7 mile course at an average speed of 311 mph. Much to the delight of the German Propaganda Ministry, the Ju 88V-5 had demonstrated speeds comparable to contemporary British fighters.

The Ju 88V-6 (D-ASCY), which made its first flight on 18 June 1938, was the first production prototype. Powered by 1,200 hp Jumo 211B-1 engines driving four bladed propellers, the Ju 88V-6 retained the upper canopy and ventral gondola introduced on the Ju 88V-4. The landing gear, however, was completely revised. The twin-oleo landing gear legs were replaced by a single main landing gear leg which rotated through 90 degrees to lie flat inside the rear of the engine nacelle. The new landing gear design allowed the exterior landing gear doors to be redesigned with a shallower, less bulged profile. Provision was made for a third 7.9MM MG 15 machine gun carried in a flexible mount in the starboard windscreen. Loaded weight of the Ju 88V-6 was 22,590 pounds, 3,850 pounds heavier than the Ju 88V-3.

The RLM was satisfied with the Ju 88V-6 and ordered additional developmental prototypes and ten pre-production aircraft under the designation Ju 88A-0. The Ju 88V-7 (first flown in September of 1938) was essentially similar to the Ju 88V-6 and served as the second production prototype. Later in its career, the JU 88V-7 would be instrumental in the development of the Ju 88C fighter. To satisfy an RLM demand for dive bombing capability, the Ju 88V-8 and V-9 (both flown in October of 1938) were modified to incorporate underwing dive brakes and an automatic pullout system. In its final form, this system functioned much like the system installed in the Junkers Ju 87 Stuka. After sighting his target, the pilot activated the system which automatically extended the underwing dive brakes, set the elevator trim, and started the dive (usually at an angle of 50-60 degrees). When the bombs were dropped (at approximately 3,300 feet) the elevator trim would automatically reset for safe pullout with the pilot manually retracting the dive brakes when the aircraft leveled out.

The Ju 88V-10 was the last prototype (first flown in February of 1939) and featured four external ETC electrically operated bomb racks, which were later interchangeable with the ETC 250 (250kg), ETC 500 (500kg) and ETC 1000 (1,000 kg) bomb racks, mounted two under each wing, inboard of the engine nacelles. These racks were equipped with explosive bolts that allowed them to be jettisoned in an emergency — a feature which later proved to be somewhat unreliable.

Ju 88A-0

Incorporating the changes progressively introduced and tested on the preceeding prototypes, the ten pre-production Ju 88A-0s began to leave the Junkers assembly line in March of 1939. The crew positions were finalized with the pilot and aft-gunner/radio-operator seated back to back on the port side of the cockpit on a stepped cockpit 'box' which also housed the control cables. The bombardier (who also doubled as forward gunner) was seated next to and slightly below the pilot, while a rear facing folding seat was provided for the ventral gunner/flight-engineer low on the starboard side of the cockpit. The gunner was forbidden from riding in the *Bodenwanne* (bottom tub) during taxi, take off, or landing, since the position could be easily crushed in the event of an accident. In an emergency, the bombardier could fly the aircraft by means of a *Hilfssteuer* (assist steer) control stick.

For dive bombing attacks, a 'BZA' dive bombing sight could be mounted on the upper port windshield framing. The pilot could judge the proper dive angle by using color coded lines etched on the pilot's port sliding window, as well as a 50 degree horizon line which was etched around the entire canopy. Defensive armament now consisted of three 7.92MM Rheinmetall-Borsig MG 15 machine guns, one mounted in the forward windscreen in front of the pilot, one in the rear of the 'greenhouse' canopy, and a third mounted at the rear of the ventral gondola.

Landing Gear

For emergency ditching, a life raft was located in a compartment on the rear fuselage decking. The inflatable raft was equipped with an emergency radio, oars, and a manually operated auxiliary air pump. An external tow line, which extended along the fuselage spine from the rear of the canopy to the raft compartment, provided access to the raft after ditching. Two fuel jettison pipes housed in a fairing at the base of the rudder allowed the pilot to quickly dump fuel before ditching (or crash landing). Two self sealing rubberized bladder fuel tanks were installed in each wing, one inboard (110 gallons) and one outboard (107 gallons) of the engine nacelles. For long range missions an auxiliary 316 gallon fuel tank could be carried in the forward bomb bay and a similar tank of 175 gallons could be installed in the rear bomb bay.

The wing de-icing system consisted of a hollow 'D' wing leading edge. Warm air, drawn from behind the radiators and exhaust stacks, was blown along the hollow wing leading edge to the wingtip, where it was discharged into the interior of the wing, raising both the internal and external temperature. The hot air could be discharged when not needed through vents on the side of the nacelle just in front of the wing leading edge. The de-icers on the horizontal stabilizer were conventional inflatable rubber leading edge de-icers.

The ten pre-production Ju 88A-0s were assigned to *Erprobungskommando* 88, a unit formed specifically to evaluate the Ju 88 under operational conditions and develop training techniques. This unit would later provide a pool of experienced pilots to form the first operational Ju 88 unit in August of 1939.

The revised main landing gear of the Ju 88 retracted rearward with the wheels rotating through a 90 degree arc to lay flat in the wheel well. The rear gear doors opened only during retraction or extension and were closed when the aircraft was on the ground.

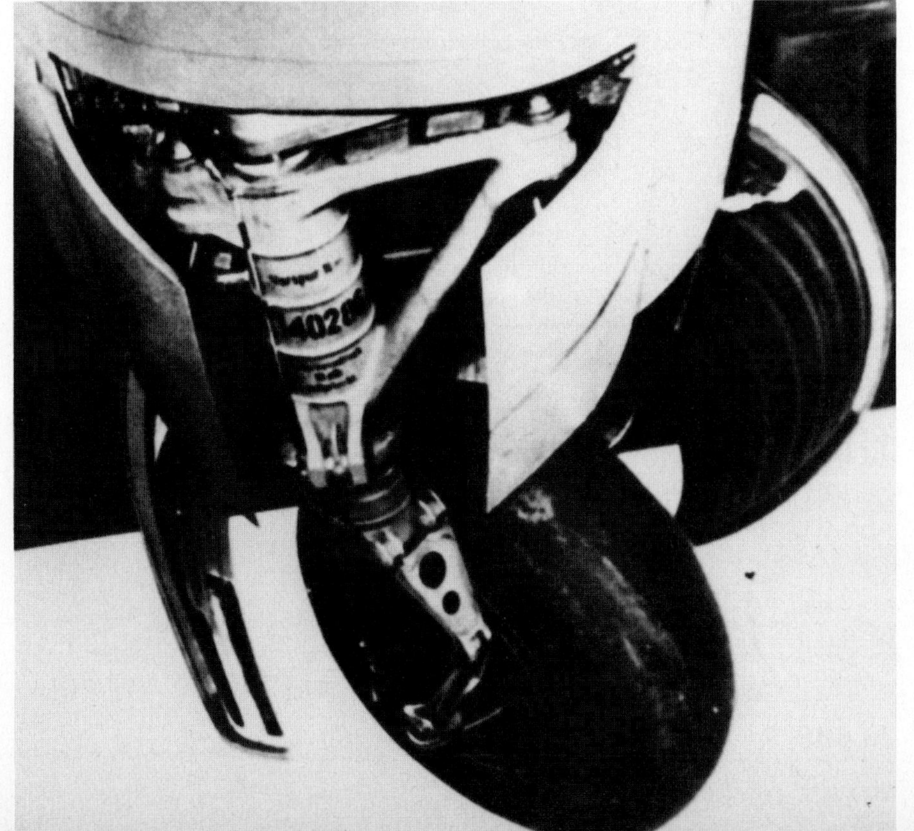

The ten pre-production Ju 88A-0s were assigned to *Erprobungskommando* 88, which evaluated the new bomber under combat conditions and evolved training techniques. This aircraft carries an early five character factory code.

Final Prototype Additions

Ju 88V-6/A-0

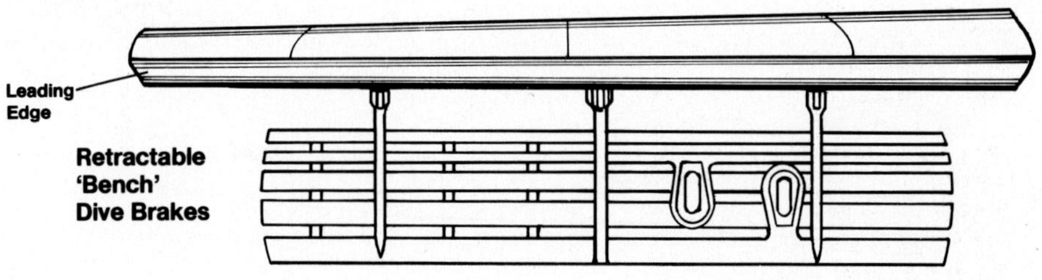

Fuel Dump Outlet Ju 88V-10/A-0

ETC Underwing Racks Ju-88V-10/A-0

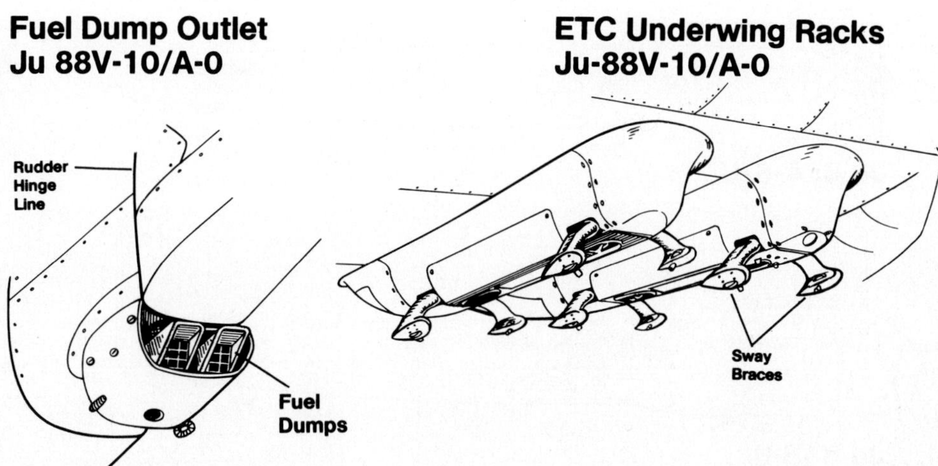

Development

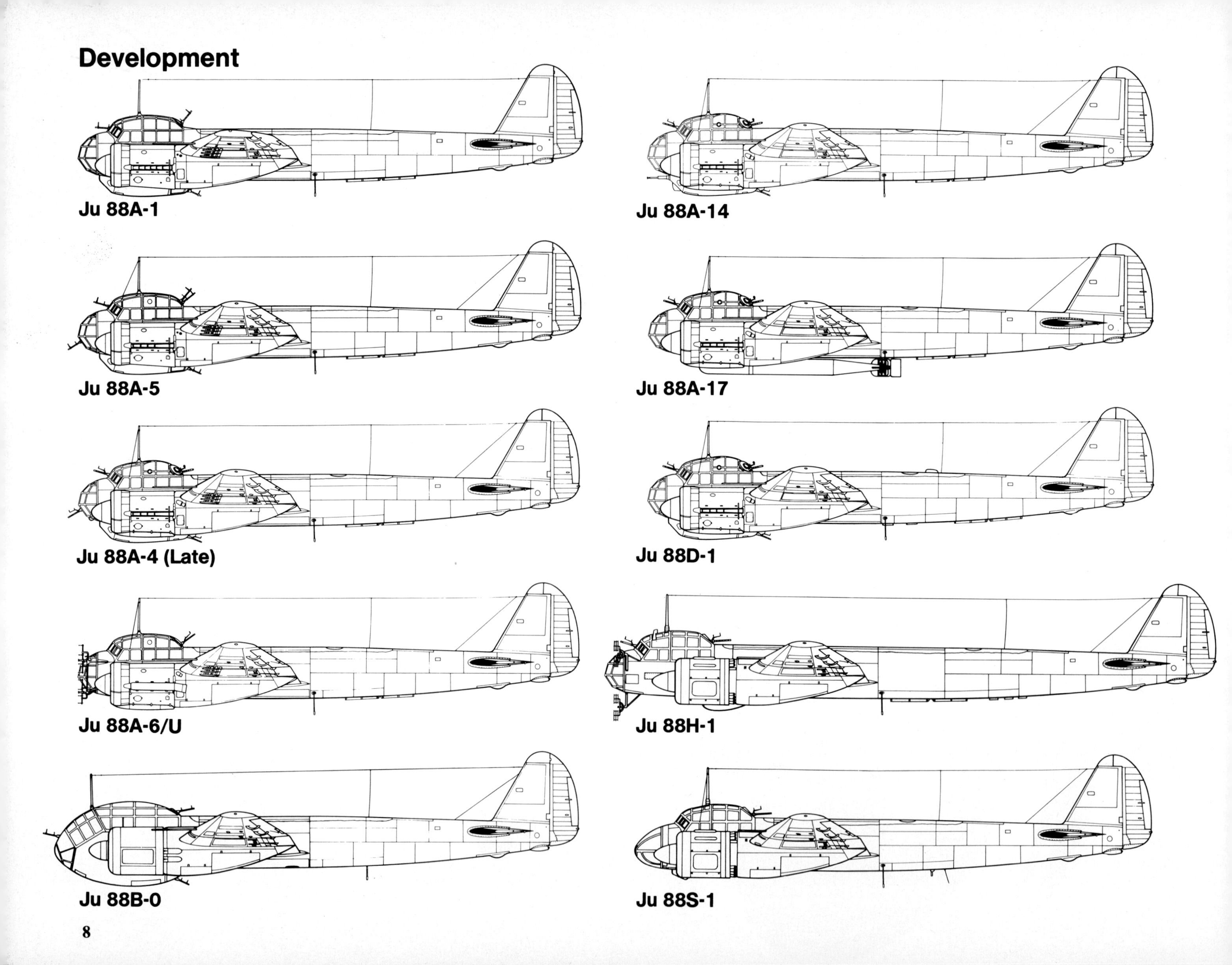

Ju 88A-1

Production of the Ju 88 was shared by a number of widely separated sub-contractors including Arado, Dornier, Heinkel, Henschel, and Volkswagen. The Ju 88A-1 differed from the pre-production Ju 88A-O in that the four bladed propellers carried by the Ju 88A-O were replaced by three bladed variable pitch VDM propellers. Additionally, the under fuselage trailing antenna mast carried on the starboard side of the Ju 88A-0 was moved to the port side of the fuselage just behind and below the trailing edge of the wing. Eventually the ten pre-production Ju 88A-0s were modified to Ju 88A-1 standards with sixty-nine Ju 88A-1s being produced during 1939.

The Ju 88A-1 initially suffered a number of teething troubles. The aircraft's highly stressed structure required cautious use of the slatted underwing dive brakes and violent maneuvers were prohibited. Several landing gear failures were experienced, and crews were cautioned to follow the factory prescribed weight and balance diagrams exactly to avoid accidents.

On long range missions the Ju 88A-1 could carry a 1,102 pound bomb load 2,285 miles (with a maximum fuel load). For short range missions the Ju 88A-1 could lift a bomb load of 5,291 pounds to a range of 782 miles (with minimum fuel). In addition to the two auxiliary bomb bay tanks, the Ju 88A-1 could also carry two 237.6 gallon external drop tanks on the underwing ETC racks. To insure a reasonable combat radius under combat conditions, the forward auxiliary bomb-bay fuel tank was usually installed with the internal bomb load being carried in the rear bomb-bay. The bomb racks could accommodate a variety of weapons including high explosive, armor-piercing, and incendiary bombs. Alternative loads included 1,100 pound aerial mines which were parachuted into the water at speeds below 185 mph at a maximum altitude of 300 feet. Maximum gross weight (according to Junkers figures) was 27,116 pounds with a maximum fuel load and minimum bomb load.

Defensive armament was the same as that carried by the Ju 88A-0. The windscreen mounted MG 15 could be stabilized with a retractable barrel lock which was installed immediately in front of the windscreen. The barrel lock allowed the pilot to operate the gun as a fixed forward firing machine gun with the aid of a Revi reflector gun sight mounted on the instrument panel.

Top speed for an empty Ju 88A-1 was 280 mph at 18,050 feet, with a cruising speed between 217-230 mph. Radio equipment installed consisted of an FuG 10 HF transceiver, FuG 16 VHF transceiver, and an FuBl 2 blind landing field approach radio, which utilized a long 'rack' antenna mounted under the fuselage.

By August of 1939 elements of *Erprobungskommando* 88 had been re-organized into I/*Kampfgeschwader* 25 to receive the first production Ju 88A-1s. Equipped with a mix of Ju 88A-0s and Ju 88A-1s I/KG 25 was redesignated to I/KG 30 on 22 September 1939, and was based at Jever. Simultaneously a training unit, *Lehrgruppe-Ju 88,* was formed at Greifswald to train aircrews for future combat units.

On 26 September 1939, I/KG 30 flew its first operational mission with the Ju 88. Four aircraft on detachment at Westerland/Sylt airfield staged an attack against British naval forces in the North Sea. During this attack, aircrews reported that the British aircraft carrier HMS ARK ROYAL was believed to have been hit by a 1,102 pound bomb and the battleship HMS HOOD also hit. Contrary to the claims of the Nazi Propaganda Ministry, HMS ARK ROYAL was not hit and none of the other ships were seriously damaged because of dud bombs.

In October, I/KG 30 mounted a number of anti-shipping patrols over the North Sea and flew missions against British naval bases, however, these attacks met with limited success. On 16 October the Ju 88A-1 made its first appearance over the British Isles in an attack against the British naval base at the Firth of Forth. Two Ju 88s, including the aircraft of *Gruppenkommandeur, Hptm* Pohle, were shot down by Spitfires of No 602 and 603 Squadrons, Royal Air Force. The attacking force did manage to damage the cruiser HMS EDINBURGH, destroyer HMS MOHAWK, and score a hit (with a dud bomb) on the

Ju 88A-1 fuselages nearing completion on the Junkers' assembly line during 1939 would be finished in camouflage colors and factory codes before the wings were attached. The ball and socket wing attachments are visible on the fuselage sides.

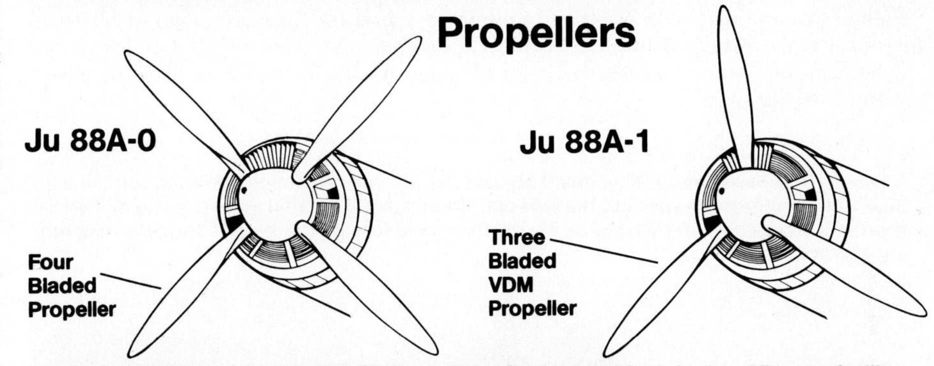

A pair of Ju 88A-1s and a Ju 87B-1 Stuka undergo final assembly at Junkers' Dessau facility. The Ju 88s are camouflaged in a splinter pattern of Black Green (70) and Dark Green (71) uppersurfaces over Light Blue (65) undersurfaces, the standard factory paint scheme.

cruiser HMS SOUTHAMPTON. By the early spring of 1940 I/KG 30 had been brought to full *Geschwader* strength (three *Gruppen* with a total of eighty-four Ju 88A-1s). Three other units KG 51, KG 4, and *Lehrgeschwader* 1 (Operational Training Wing 1) were in the process of re-equipping with the Ju 88.

On 10 May 1940 when the *Blitzkrieg* was launched against France and the Low Countries these units were still in the process of conversion and the Ju 88's participation was limited. By *Adlertag* (Eagle Day — 13 August 1940) the official beginning of the 'Battle of Britain,' KG 51 was up to full strength, III/KG 4 had completed conversion, and elements of KG 1, KG 54, and KG 40 had also re-equipped or partially formed with Ju 88A-1s. During the 'Battle of Britain', Ju 88 formations achieved some impressive results, particularly against RAF airfields. The Ju 88, however, despite its maneuverability and high speed, did not escape the punishment inflicted on German bomber formations by RAF fighters.

Among the factors contributing to the high loss rate suffered by *Luftwaffe* bomber formations was a lack of sufficient defensive armament and armor protection. In response, the first of many cockpit modifications appeared on the Ju 88A-1. Interior armor plate was added to the rear of the canopy, and the rotating plexiglass gun mounts were replaced with armored gun mounts with square armor glass windows. To improve defensive firepower, late Ju 88A-1s had the single rear canopy gun replaced by two MG 15s mounted side by side in the rear canopy. Single MG 15s were mounted in both sides of the canopy and the pilots forward firing machine gun was supplemented by an MG 15 in a pivoting mount installed in the 'beetle's-eye' nose for use by the bombardier.

By late Autumn of 1940 the 'Battle of Britain' had ended — in a victory for the RAF Fighter Command. The Ju 88A-1 had completed its first and final campaign where it was commited in substantial numbers. While a number of Ju 88A-1s would continue to serve, most *Luftwaffe* bomber *Gruppen* began phasing out the Ju 88A-1 in favor of newer variants of the Ju 88.

Range	1260 km (782.5 Miles)	2340 km (1,453 Miles)	2900 km (1,801 Miles)	3680 km (2285.25 Miles)
Fuel	1221 kg (2,692 lbs.)	2106 kg (4,643 lbs.)	2609 kg (5,752 lbs.)	3263 kg (7,193 lbs.)
Bomb Load	2400 kg (5,291 lbs.)	1500 kg (3,307 lbs.)	1000 kg (2,204 lbs.)	500 kg (1,102 lbs.)
Flying Weight	11900 kg (26,234.74 lbs.)	12000 kg (26,455 lbs.)	12100 kg (26,675 lbs.)	12300 kg (27,116 lbs.)
JFM 1939	Range by Various Equipment Conditions Ju 88			JFM 123

Reproduction of Junkers Factory Chart showing balances of Fuel, Bomb load and effective Range. This Chart was dated "JFM 1939" indicating that it applies to the Ju 88A-1.

FuG 10 Underfuselage Trailing Antenna Mast

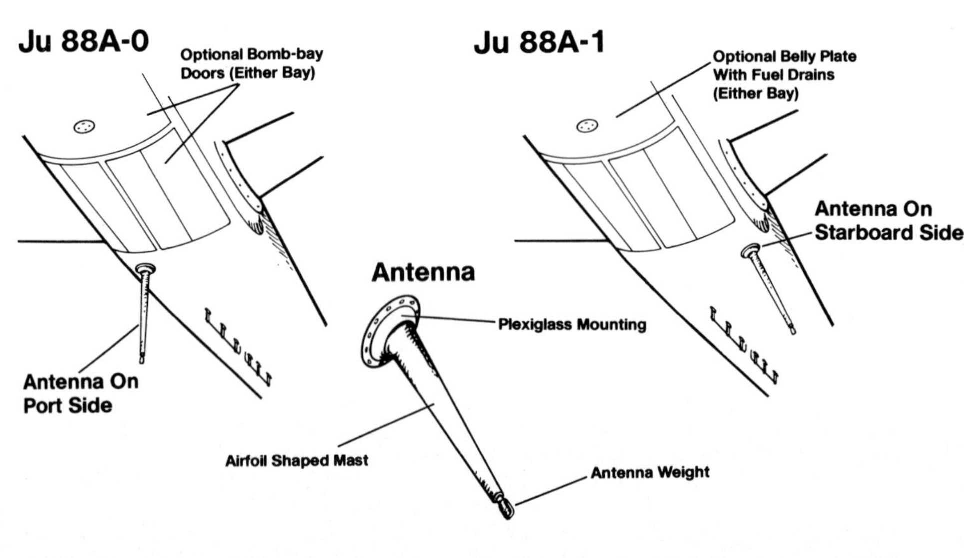

A *Luftwaffe Schwarzmann* (Blackman) adjusts the cockpit radio mast antenna wire on a Ju 88A-1 of *Kampfgeschwader* 30, the first operational Ju 88 combat unit. The line etched on the forward canopy is the 50 degree horizon line used to align the aircraft during dive bombing attacks.

An early production Ju 88A-1, Yellow '10' (VA+EH), on a factory acceptance flight prior to deilvery to the *Luftwaffe*. After delivery, the factory codes were replaced with unit codes. Despite a number of early problems, the Ju 88A-1 quickly gained a reputation as a reliable and rugged aircraft.

Aircrews of 7.*Staffel*/KG 51 are briefed for their next mission under the wing of 9K+LR, an early production Ju 88A-1. The trailing antenna mast and rack antenna for the FuBl 2 blind landing approach radio are visible under the center fuselage. The spinners, letter 'L' on the fuselage, and *Werk-Nummer* on the fin are in White. The retractable underwing dive brake is visible. (Smithsonian)

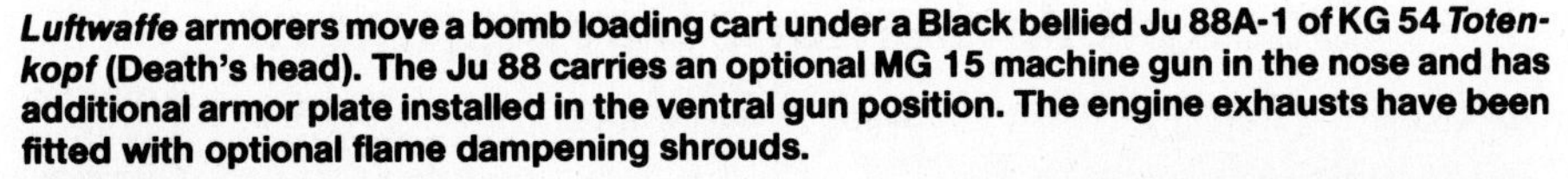

Luftwaffe armorers move a bomb loading cart under a Black bellied Ju 88A-1 of KG 54 *Totenkopf* (Death's head). The Ju 88 carries an optional MG 15 machine gun in the nose and has additional armor plate installed in the ventral gun position. The engine exhausts have been fitted with optional flame dampening shrouds.

A Ju 88A-1 with a full external bomb load of four 250 kg (551 pound) bombs awaits sundown to begin a night mission against England. When daylight operations over England proved too costly, the *Luftwaffe* shifted to night bombing. The undersurfaces and White areas around the national insignias have been overpainted with Flat Black. Staggered side canopy MG 15s have been fitted.

Two crewmen board a Ju 88A-1 of 3./KG 51 *Edelweiss* on an airfield in France. The oval window at the front of the ventral gondola is the aiming window for the Lotfe bombsight, while the window next to the gondola provided a degree of downward vision for the pilot. The optional side canopy MG 15 machine guns proved difficult to use in the cramped cockpit of the Ju 88.

Ventral Armament Development

Ju 88A-1 (Early)

Rotating
MG 15
Gun Mount

Ju 88A-1 (Late)

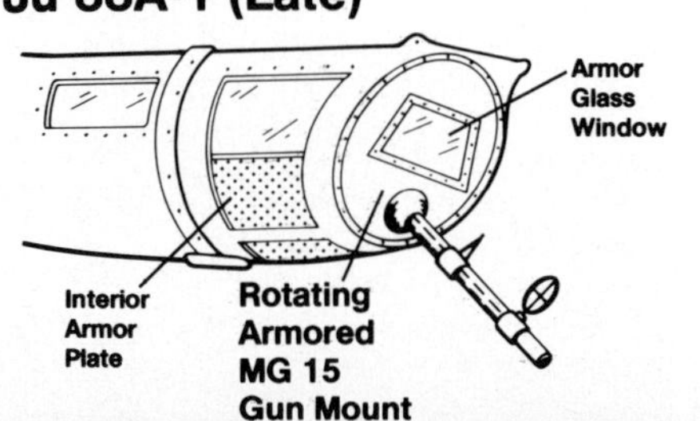

Late production Ju 88A-1s replaced the single rotating rear cockpit gun mount with two MG 15 machine guns in simple flexible gun mounts. The lack of cockpit armor plate and gunsights indicates that work on the rear canopy conversion has not been completed. The White background of the unit insignia indicates this bomber is assigned to I/KG 30.

Cockpit Armament Development

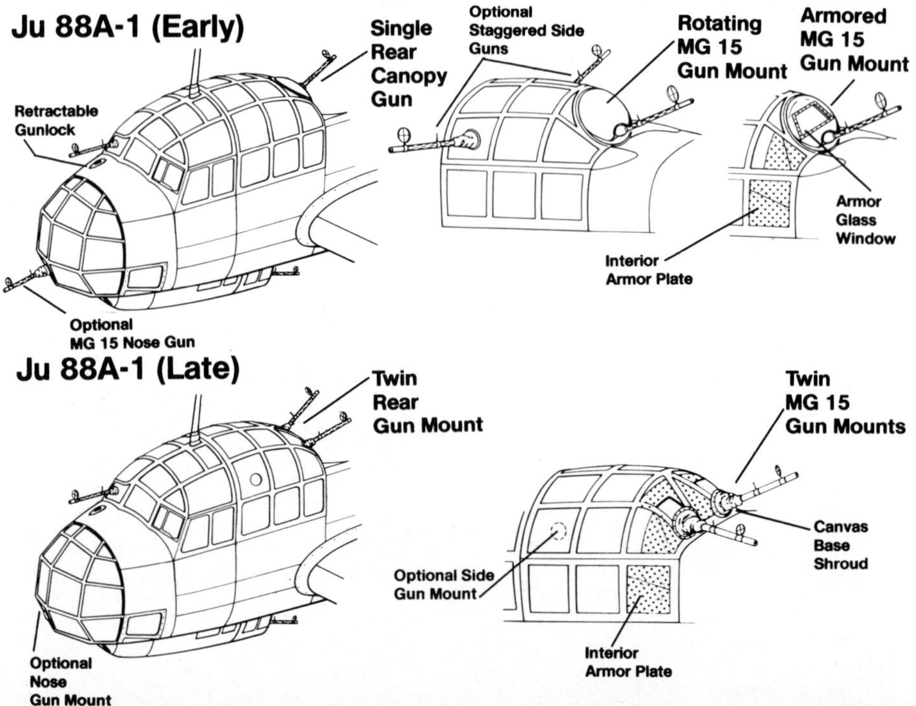

A Ju 88A awaits recovery after a crash landing. The rear canopy was jettisoned in three parts, first the top, then the two side panels. The pilot's seat has a slanted armored head rest while the tubular head rest frame on the radio operator's seat folded downward to allow access to a map case located on the back of the pilot's seat.

Ju 88A-1 Front Cockpit

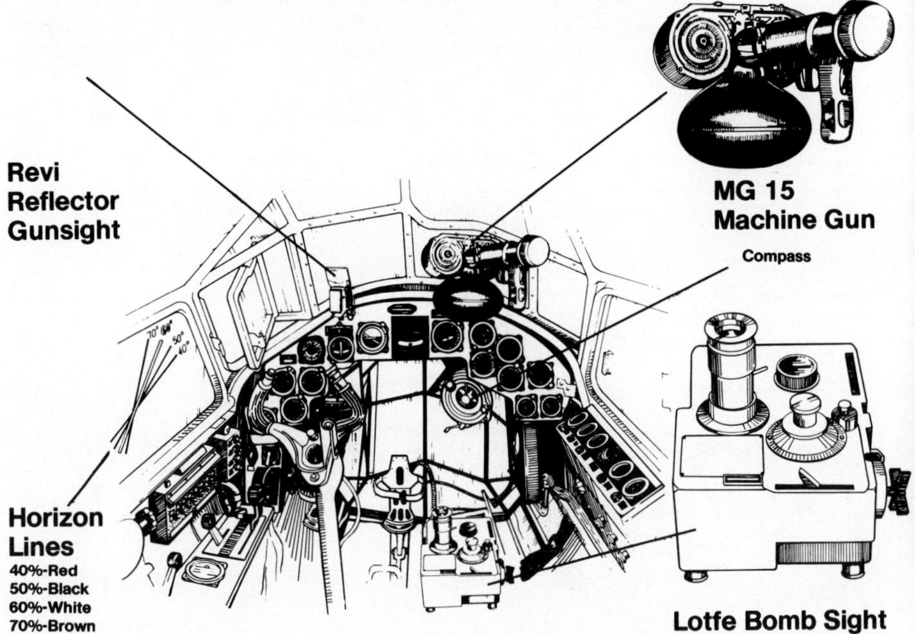

The front cockpit of a Ju 88A-1. Flight instruments were grouped on a curved instrument panel with the compass mounted low on the right side of the panel. The Revi reflector gunsight and retractable gun lock allowed the pilot to fire the forward MG 15 as a fixed gun, while the ball-and-socket mount allowed the bombardier/gunner to use the weapon as a flexible gun. The Lotfe bombsight is located to the right and below the pilot.

Ju 88A-2/Ju 88A-3

Externally identical to the Ju 88A-1, the Ju 88A-2 had the 1,200 hp Jumo 211B-1 engines replaced by improved 1,200 hp Jumo 211G-1 engines. Additionally the wings were modified to accept a Walter rocket assist take off pod under each wing. The 1,100 pound thrust Walter rocket pods were installed under the wings outboard of the engine nacelles and provided the Ju 88A-2 with extra power for take off when operating with a heavy load.

The rockets, referred to both as *R-Geräte* (for *Rauchgeräte*, Smoke Devices)or *Startraketen* (start rockets), were completely self contained. The upper framework mounted to the wing by three hooks. These hooks fastened into attachment points on the underside of the wing. The front attachment points were accessible through openings in the underwing dive brakes, while the third point was located in front of the trailing edge flaps. The forward portion of each pod contained a recovery parachute which opened after the pod was jettisoned. Each re-usable rocket pod provided approximately twenty-five to thirty seconds of usable thrust. Special ground crews were responsible for the installation and recovery of the 'ATO' (assist take off) pods and these rocket packs became an optional feature on practically all subsequent Ju 88A variants.

Ju 88A-3

In order to provide conversion training for Ju 88 crews, the *Luftwaffe* requested a specialized training variant of the Ju 88A-1. Based on the Ju 88A-1 airframe, a dedicated trainer was developed under the designation Ju 88A-3. The Ju 88A-3 featured a complete set of instruments, separate steering yokes, and throttle controls for both the instructor and student. Ju 88A-3s usually carried a crew of three and were unarmed, with the gun mounts being replaced by transparent 'bubble' windows.

(Right) *Luftwaffe* mechanics service the port Jumo engine of a Ju 88A. The large duct above the exhausts brought air to the engine from the faceplate air intakes, while the three small *anzeigengeräte* (indicator guages) were visible to the pilot through small circular windows in the cowling side panels. (Smithsonian)

(Below) The 1,100 pound thrust Walter rocket pods under the wings of this Ju 88A-2 of KG 51 allowed the bomber to lift heavy bomb loads from short fields. The parachute on the front of the rocket pods lowered the pod to the ground after it was jettisoned allowing the pod to be recovered and reused later. (USAF)

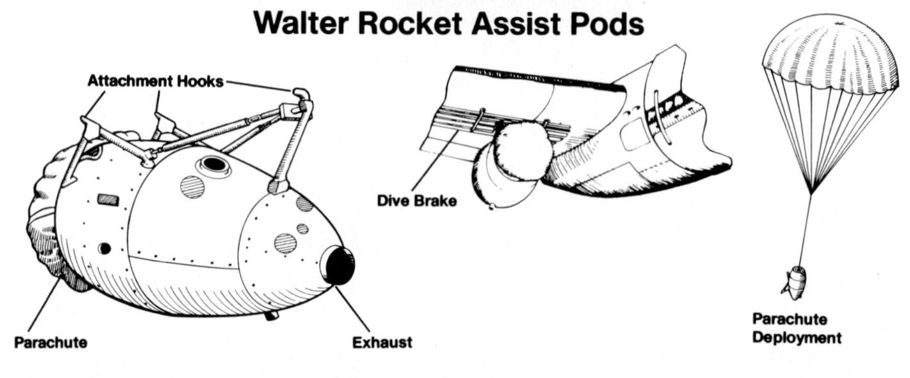

Ju 88A-5

In early 1940 Junkers began work on an improved variant of the Ju 88, the Ju 88A-4, which was to be powered by the 1,400 hp Jumo 211F or J engine. However, delays in the development of the Jumo 211F and J engines led the RLM to order an interim variant incorporating some of the improvements planned for the Ju 88A-4 under the designation Ju 88A-5.

The Ju 88A-5 was based on the Ju 88A-1 airframe modified with extended outer wing panels that had been designed for the Ju 88A-4. The new wing increased the span to 65 feet 7 ½ inches and replaced the fabric covered ailerons with metal skinned 'inset' ailerons. Defensive armament remained as on late production Ju 88A-1s, although a number of early Ju 88A-5s were delivered with the single rear cockpit gun mount of the early A-1. The maximum gross weight of the Ju 88A-5 was increased by 331 pounds over the Ju 88A-1 to 27,447 pounds.

The Ju 88A-5 could carry an additional ETC 250 bomb rack under each wing, outboard of the engine nacelle. These racks were capable of carrying two 550 pound bombs, but were seldom used operationally. Like the Ju 88A-1, the A-5 was powered by two 1,200 hp Jumo 211B engines, however, late production A-5s were powered by either the 1,200 hp Jumo 211G-1 or H-1 engines. Radio equipment of the Ju 88A-5 was updated with the inclusion of an FuG 25 IFF (identification friend or foe) transceiver. On late production machines modifications were made to the vertical tail and canopy antenna mast aerials.

The first Ju 88A-5s began leaving the assembly line during the spring of 1940, entering squadron service in time for the 'Battle of Britain', where they fought alongside Ju 88A-1s. Although the Ju 88A-5 offered no significant improvement in power over the earlier Ju 88A-1, it was popular with its crews because of the improved control response and maneuverability produced by the increased wing span. By late 1940, the Ju 88A-5 was steadily replacing the A-1 in *Luftwaffe* bomber squadrons. During the 1941 campaigns against Yugoslavia and Greece, the Ju 88A-5 was the primary variant in service. So complete was the changeover from the short span Ju 88A-1 to the long span Ju 88A-5, that only a few A-1s remained in service by mid-1941.

As the Ju 88A-5 was introduced into squadron service, a number of 'retired' Ju 88A-1s were returned to Junkers where they were re-manufactured to A-5 standards. One well known example was a Ju 88A-5 *Stammkennzeichen* (side code) M2+MK (Werk-Nr. 6073), which was captured intact by the British at Chivenor Aerodrome on 27 November 1941. By studying the manufacture's data plates the British learned that the bomber had been originally built as a Ju 88A-1 in March of 1940 and had been later re-built to A-5 standards.

Ju 88A-5 (Late)

Lessons learned in combat dictated a number of changes in the defensive armament of the Ju 88A-5, changes that would ultimately become standardized on the later Ju 88A-4. To expand the field of fire of the rear canopy machine guns and provide more interior space for the gunner, a double bulged rear canopy was introduced. Each rear canopy bulge tapered down to an armored rotating gun mount. Two different style gun mounts were carried on the Ju 88A-5, although both were identical in operation. The early mount featured square armor glass sighting panels while the later mount had kidney shaped armor glass sighting panels. The weapons fitted were usually 7.9MM MG 15 machine guns, although a number of Ju 88A-5s were fitted with the faster firing 7.9MM MG 81J machine gun.

A number of Ju 88A-5s also had the ventral gondola gun position changed. The early rear gun tub/entry hatch with its circular gun mount was replaced by either a Bola (*Bodenlafette* — ventral gun mount) 39C or Bola 39D VE gun tub. These gun tubs were shallower in depth and both were equipped with horizontal gun traverse and horse shoe shaped interior armor plate. Both units (the 39D VE differed from the 39C in the type of elevated gun sight installed) usually mounted a single MG 15, with the option of installing either an MG 81 or 13MM MG 131 in place of the MG 15. On a small number of aircraft, the ventral position was retro-fitted with the Bola 81Z, which featured the same configuration as the Bola 39, but mounted a 7.9MM MG 81Z *Zwilling* (twin) machine gun with an elevated VE gun sight.

Ju 88A s of KG 77 enroute to British targets during the summer of 1940. The aircraft in the background is a Ju 88A-5, identifed by the long span wings, inset ailerons, and twin rear canopy gun position. The single rear canopy gun mount on the aircraft in foreground suggests that it is a Ju 88A-1, however, a number of early Ju 88A-5s also retained the single rear canopy gun position.

Ultimately, these diverse armament options (both factory installed and field modified) would appear on service Ju 88A-5s in various combinations, including 'hybrid' configurations that mixed early and late armament options. The most common late production configuration was a single forward firing windscreen mounted MG 15, two MG 15s in double bulged rear canopy mounts, and one MG 15 in an early style ventral gun tub. The Ju 88A-5 had a total ammunition capacity (with MG 15s) of 1,500 rounds.

Production of the Ju 88A-5 continued until late 1941, overlapping the Ju 88A-4. A total of 3,962 Ju 88A series bombers were produced between 1940 and 1941. The precise number of Ju 88A-5s (new built or rebuilt A-1s) remains undetermined, however, sufficent quantities of the A-5 were produced to re-equip every *Kampfgeschwader* which operated the Ju 88.

Wing Development

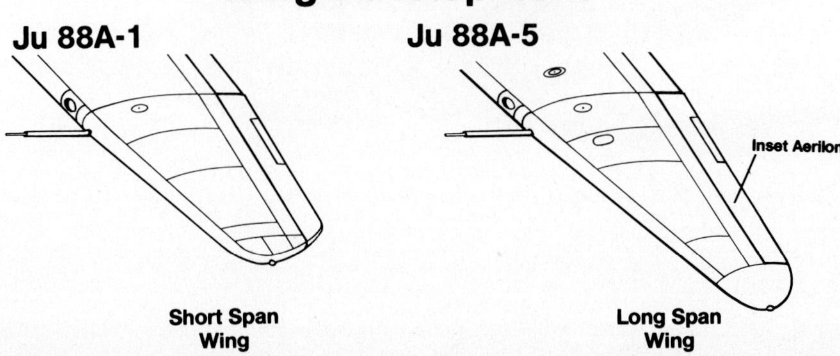

This early Ju 88A-5 carries the cow astride a bomb insignia of 4./KG 1. The opening in the upper canopy center section is a gun mount for an optional side mounted MG 15 machine gun. A number of Ju 88A-5s also featured an exterior 'stop bar' on the canopy framing below the gun mount to prevent the gunner from firing into the engine nacelle.

Bombs have been stacked in preparation for loading on a Ju 88A-5 of III/LG 1 at a desert base in North Africa. The White fuselage band was a recognition aid introduced for the Mediterranean and North African theatre of operations. The White fuselage code letter 'F' has been retouched with Black where it overlaps the fuselage band.

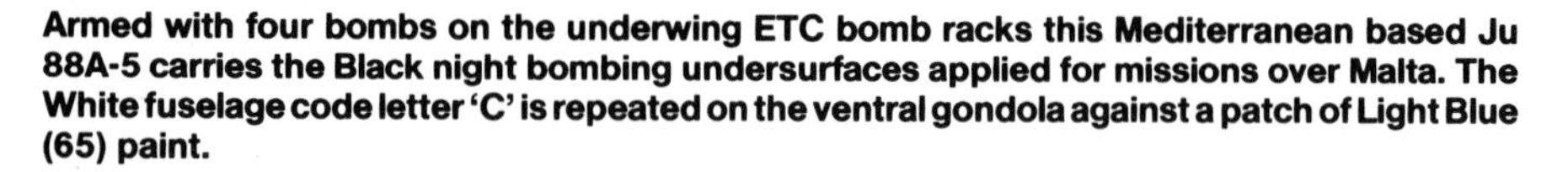

Armed with four bombs on the underwing ETC bomb racks this Mediterranean based Ju 88A-5 carries the Black night bombing undersurfaces applied for missions over Malta. The White fuselage code letter 'C' is repeated on the ventral gondola against a patch of Light Blue (65) paint.

The sheared propeller shaft on the starboard engine of this Ju 88A-5 of I/LG 1 suggests that the aircraft threw its propeller in flight. By early 1941 most Ju 88A-5s were modified with the improved double bulged rear canopy gun position which provided greater freedom of movement for the rear gunner. This installation was standardized on late production machines.

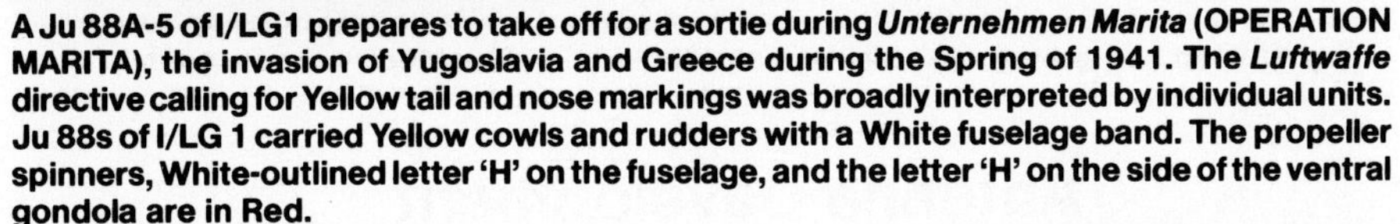

A Ju 88A-5 of I/LG1 prepares to take off for a sortie during *Unternehmen Marita* (OPERATION MARITA), the invasion of Yugoslavia and Greece during the Spring of 1941. The *Luftwaffe* directive calling for Yellow tail and nose markings was broadly interpreted by individual units. Ju 88s of I/LG 1 carried Yellow cowls and rudders with a White fuselage band. The propeller spinners, White-outlined letter 'H' on the fuselage, and the letter 'H' on the side of the ventral gondola are in Red.

Ground crews load an SC 1000 (2,205 pound) bomb on a late production Ju 88A-5 of I/LG 1 on an airfield in Greece during the Spring of 1941. In keeping with the directive for Yellow identification markings, the fuselage nose below the canopy has been painted Yellow. The spinners are segmented in Dark Green and White, while the undersurfaces have been over-painted in Black for night missions. (William Hess)

Armament Development

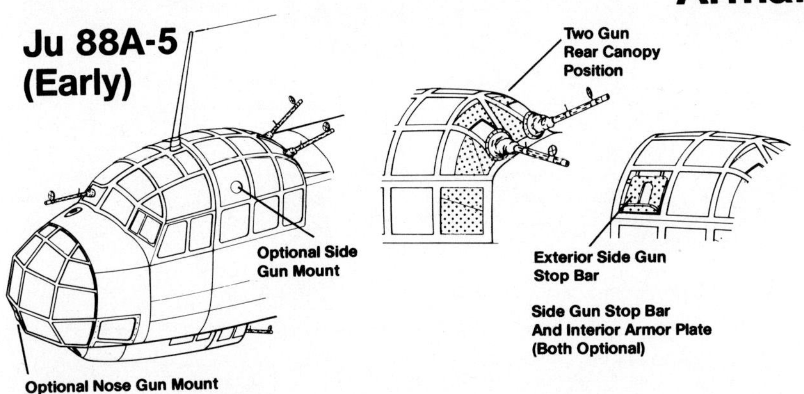

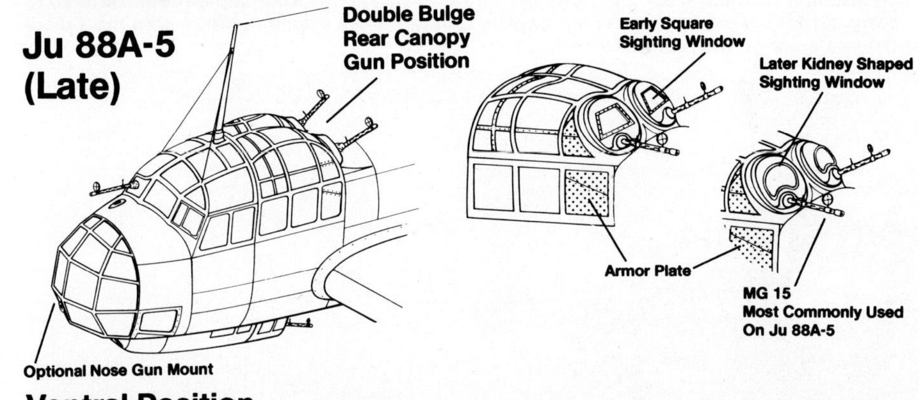

Ventral Position

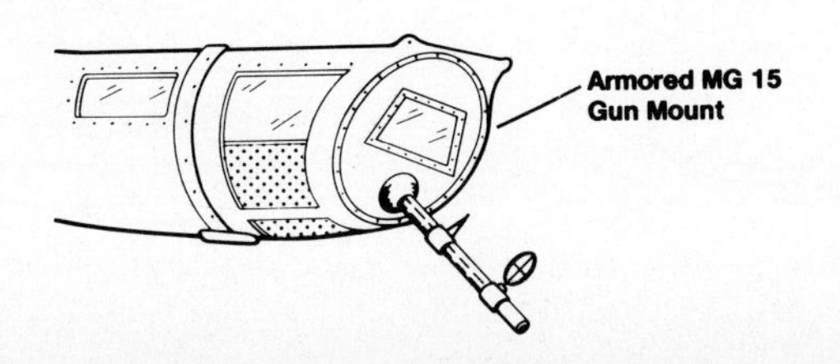

Ventral Position

Bola 39C

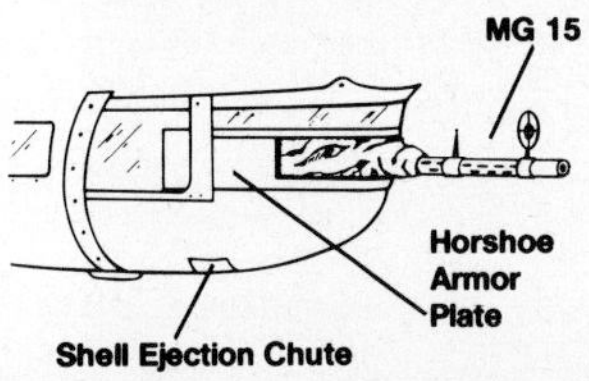

MG 15

Horshoe Armor Plate

Shell Ejection Chute

Bola 39D VE

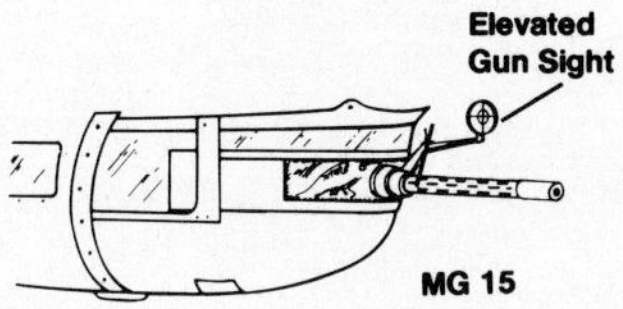

Elevated Gun Sight

MG 15

Bola 81Z (Some Ju 88A-5s)

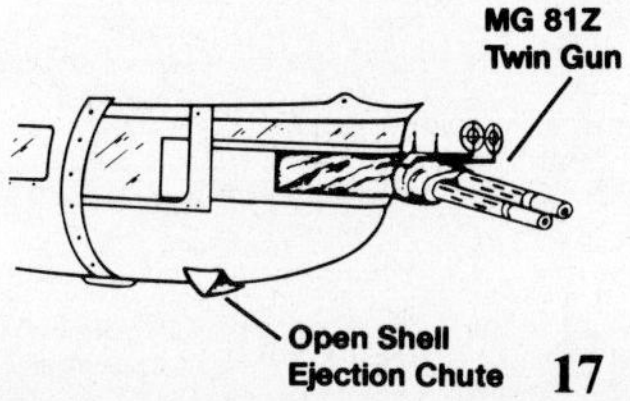

MG 81Z Twin Gun

Open Shell Ejection Chute

Although various defensive machine guns could be carried on the Ju 88A-5, the 7.9MM MG 15 machine gun was the most commonly used weapon. The triangular marking of the fuel tank filler caps are fuel octane markings which specified the type of fuel to be used when servicing the bomber.

A ground crewman refuels a late Ju 88A-5 (F1+GM, Werk-Nr. 4339) of KG 76 on a Russian airfield. The rubber bumpers on the fuel hose prevented surface damage to the wing during servicing. The last two letters of the fuselage code have been repeated on the fin in White as an identification aid.

Ju 88A-5s of III/KG 77 parked on a grass airstrip in Russia during the Summer of 1941. Theatre markings include Yellow fuselage bands and wingtips. 3Z+AR and 3Z+FR are equipped with 500 liter containers on the ETC wing racks; these containers could be used to carry either fuel or supplies. The propeller spinners were tipped in White with the Yellow *Gruppe* color on the rear half.

Antenna Development

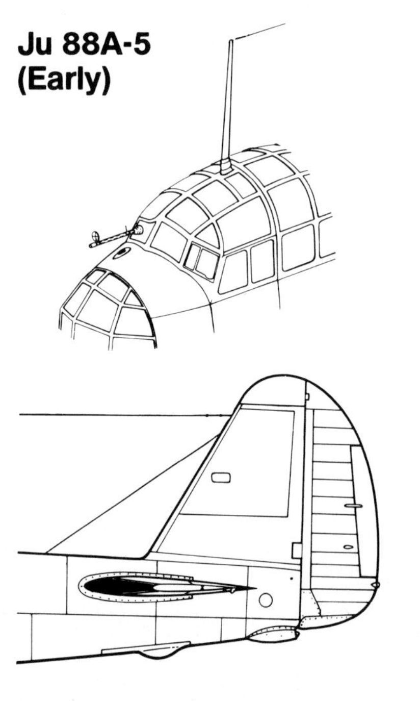

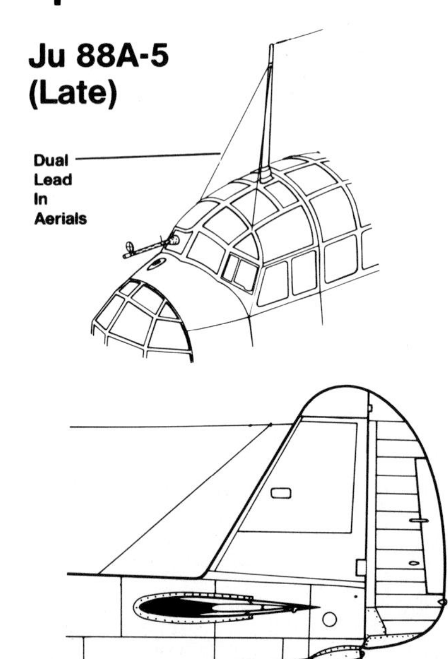

Ju 88A-5s of I/KG 806 and KG 30 parked on an Eastern Front airfield during 1941. KG 806 was one of several *Küstenflieger Gruppen* (coastal flying groups) which were later redesignated as *Kampf Gruppen* (Battle groups). M7+AK of I/KG 806 has the fuselage letter 'A' in Red with a thin White outline and is fitted with the 'Bola 39' ventral gun position.

A Ju 88A-5 of KG-1 *Hindenberg* carries the temporary water based White camouflage applied to aircraft operating on the Eastern Front. This Ju 88A-5 has the late double bulged rear canopy gun position while retaining the earlier style ventral gun position. It was not uncommon to find various armament configurations on service Ju 88A-5s.

Ju 88A-4

By early 1941, sufficient quantities of the 1,400 hp Jumo 211F and 211J engines had become available to allow Junkers to begin production of the Ju 88A-4. Early production Ju 88A-4s were fitted with the Jumo 211F engine pending availability of the more reliable Jumo 211J-1 and J-2 engines. Shortly after production was started the Jumo 211J-1 became available in quantity and this engine became the designated powerplant of subsequent Ju 88A-4s.

The increased power allowed Junkers to increase armor protection, bomb load, and fuel, raising the gross weight of the Ju 88A-4 to 30,864 pounds, some 3,700 pounds heavier than the Ju 88A-1. Top speed was increased by some 15 mph and the bomb-load was increased to 7,936 pounds. The Ju 88A-4 would become the most produced variant of the Ju 88 and would be the basis for most subsequent Ju 88 variants.

The Jumo 211J engine featured a pressurized coolant system with an induction air cooler located under the rear of the engine. To accommodate this revised cooling system an asymmetrical bulged fairing was installed under the engine cowling and an additional air intake was added to the center of the lower face of the annular radiator. The thin chord VDM metal propellers were replaced by broader compressed laminated wood VS-11 propellers with enlarged spinners, however, a number of early Ju 88A-4s were delivered with VDM propellers. To improve the aerodynamics of the engine nacelles the hot air exhausts, located just ahead of the wing leading edge were covered with streamlined fairings.

Interior armor protection was improved with additional armor added to the cockpit side walls, floorboards, and ventral gondola. On early production Ju 88A-4s the pilot's seat was reinforced with extra armor plate installed on the seat back, while late production Ju 88A-4s had the seat replaced with a contoured armored seat that featured head and shoulder armor protection and an armored backplate.

The primary defensive machine gun was changed from the drum fed MG 15 to the faster firing belt fed MG 81J. Ammunition bins were installed in the cockpit which provided 750 rounds for the forward windscreen weapon, 1,000 rounds for each of the rear cockpit guns, and 1,800 rounds for the ventral MG 81Z. The ammunition bin for the windscreen gun was obliquely mounted on the inside framework of the nose. In squadron service, the nose ammuntion bin was found to block forward view for the pilot and the windscreen gun was often replaced with a drum fed MG 15 with the ammunition bin being deleted. For additional forward defense, a fifth machine gun (either an MG 15, MG 81, MG 131 or, in rare cases, an MG 81Z) could be installed in the nose gun mount, however, the nose gun mount was less frequently used as the war progressed.

Variations in armament configurations were common on service Ju 88A-4s. A number of aircraft had the windscreen MG 81 replaced with a 13MM MG 131 machine gun. A small number of late production aircraft were modified with the two rear cockpit MG 81Js replaced by a single MG 131 mounted in a rotating armored gun mount. MG 81 and MG 131 installations were usually fitted with elevated VE ring and bead sights, however, a number of MG 81s were fitted with barrel mounted ring and bead sights. Finally, small staggered ring or 'donut' gun mounts were installed in the side canopy framework, however, these optional side gun mounts were rarely used.

The fuselage bomb-bay loads (as recommended by the Ju 88A-4 handbook) included the following *Rüstzustand* (Equipment States):

Equipment State A — Up to ten 50kg (110 lb) bombs in both the forward and rear bomb-bays (twenty bombs total).

Equipment State B — Up to ten 50kg bombs in the rear bay and one 1,220 liter (322 gallon) fuel tank in the forward bay. (This was the most common configuration).

Equipment State C — One 322 gallon fuel tank in the forward bay and one 680 liter (179.5 gallon) fuel tank in the rear bay.

A pair of Ju 88A-4s of III/KG 51 *Edelweiss*, one of the first units to receive the A-4. The armament improvements which had been progressively introduced on the Ju 88A-5 became standard on the Ju 88A-4, which would become the most numerous variant of the *Schnellbomber* produced.

Defensive Armament

These Ju 88A-4s carry the Yellow shield and Red lightning bolt of KG 3 *Blitz* below the cockpit. The Ju 88A-4 had a bulged lower engine cowling to accommodate the revised cooling system of the Jumo 211J engine and VS 11 'paddle' blade propellers with enlarged spinners. Ju 88A-4s carried various armament combinations; this aircraft is fitted with an MG 15 in the starboard windshield, MG 81J with a VE elevated gun sight and cartridge ejection bin in the nose, and an MG 81Z *Zwilling* twin gun mount in the ventral position.

The external bomb load consisted of a variety of bombs up to 1,000 kgs (2,200 pounds) or 900 liter (237.6 gallon) drop tanks carried on each ETC rack, with heavier loads usually carried on the inboard rack. The optional ETC 250 bomb racks carried outboard of the engine nacelles on the Ju 88A-5 were deleted on the Ju 88A-4. To support the increased gross weight of the Ju 88A-4 the landing gear was reinforced and larger tires were fitted.

A number of improvements were introduced at various points on the Ju 88A-4 pro duction line. One of the first was the addition of an upper rudder balance which changed the shape of the rudder. For protection against Allied barrage balloon cables, a small optional cable fender was mounted on the center canopy frame of the beetle's-eye nose (this fender was also retrofitted to earlier Ju 88 variants).

Navigational equipment was updated with the installation of a *Peilgerät* EZ 6 direction finder and FuG 101 radio altimeter. The EZ 6 power operated swiveling antenna was installed in a recessed well in the upper fuselage decking. This antenna well was sealed with a flush circular plexiglass cover with a 'starburst' pattern of metalized sensing strips on the interior of the glass. The two 'T' shaped antennas for the FuG 101 radio altimeter were mounted under the port wing near the wing tip.

The Ju 88A-4's first major combat action was the invasion of Russia on 22 June 1941. KG 51 was one of the earliest units to employ the Ju 88A-4, however, by early 1942 the majority of Ju 88 equipped *Kampfgeschwader* had been re-equipped with the Ju 88A-4. By the end of 1942 there were 520 Ju 88s in frontline service — representing nearly half of the 1,135 bombers available to the *Luftwaffe*.

A 1,400 hp Junkers Jumo 211 J engine undergoes tests on an engine test rack. The induction air cooling system is located under the engine block. To accommodate this new cooling system the cowling of the Ju 88A-4 was modified with a bulged fairing under the nacelle for the cooling air ducts.

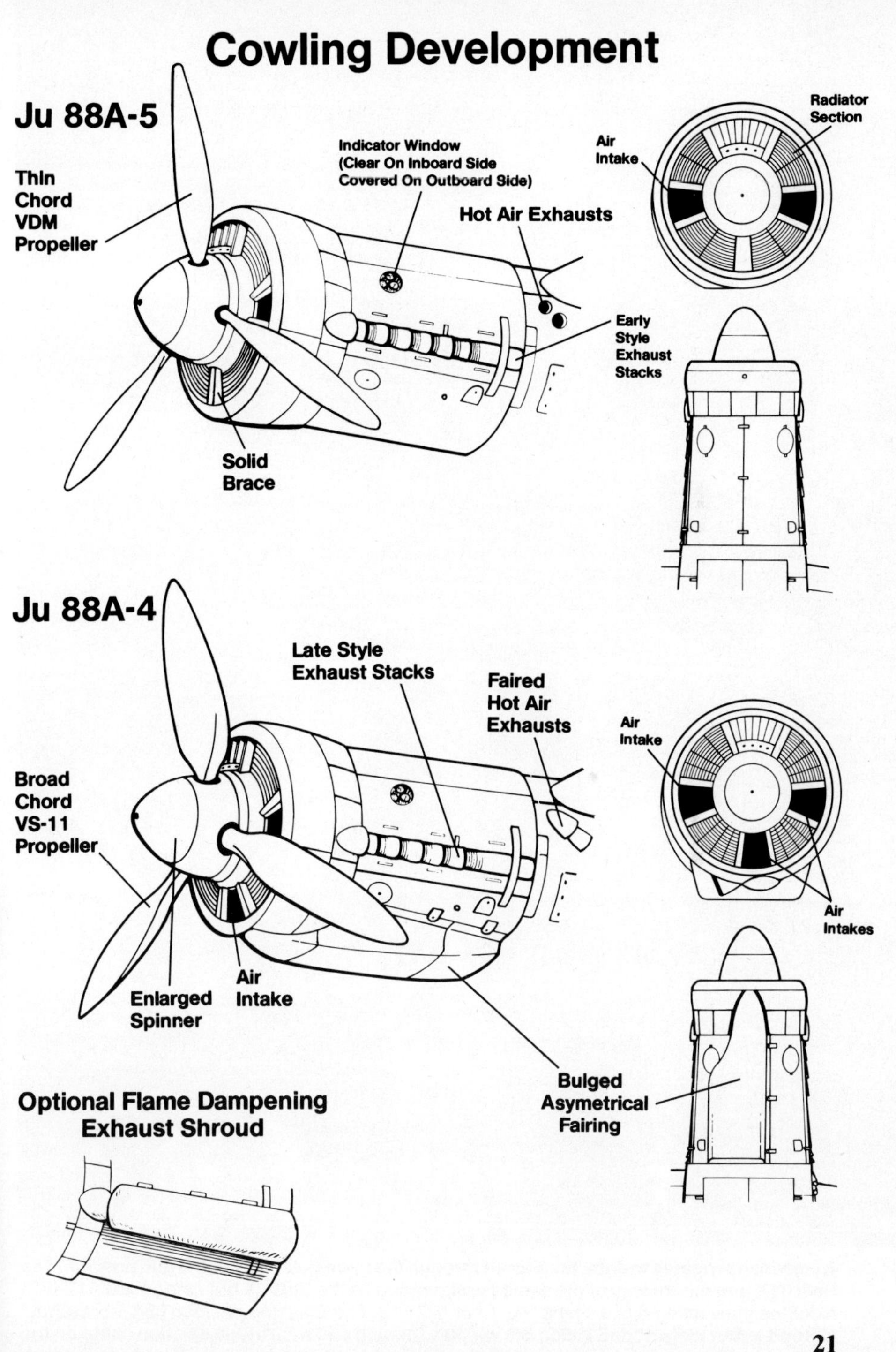

A crewman prepares to enter his aircraft through the open Bola 81Z ventral gun position. The Bola 81Z gun mount was of the same configuration as the Bola 39 but carried MG 81Z twin machine guns instead of a single MG 15 or MG 81J. The Bola gun position had 'horseshoe' shaped armor plate added inside the window framing and a cartridge ejection chute on the underside. The small pneumatic cylinder at the rear of the gun postion prevented the hatch from opening too quickly.

A gunner peers through the armor glass rotating gun mount of a Ju 88A-4 armed with MG 81J machine guns. The gunner is looking through an elevated VE gun sight, which has been fitted with an anti-glare sun shield labeled with the aircraft's *Werk Nummer*. The MG 81J was the same 7.9MM caliber as the MG 15, but had a higher rate of fire. (Gene Stafford)

Armorers load SC 50 (110 pound) bombs into the rear bomb bay of a Junkers Ju 88A-4, armed with an MG-81 machine gun in the starboard windscreen position. The gun is belt fed from an angled ammunition bin installed in the upper portion of the nose. Other Ju 88A-4s replaced the belt fed MG 81 with an optional drum fed MG 15 allowing the ammunition bin to be removed improving the pilot's forward view.

Equipped with an oxygen mask and sun glassed goggles, the radio operator/gunner searches the sky through the bulged rear canopy of a Ju 88A-4. The four bolts on the canopy behind the gunner are an optional 'donut' gun mount for a side firing gun, an option which was seldom used on the Ju 88A-4.

The pilot of this Ju 88A-4 has secured the BZA dive bombing sight to its mounting on the port windshield frame work and has drawn the canopy sun shades in preparation for a dive bomb attack. The inscription on the sight reads ***BZA nur für Sturz einschalten! Nach Sturz ausschalten!*** (BZA for dive only switch on! After dive switch off!).

Armament Development

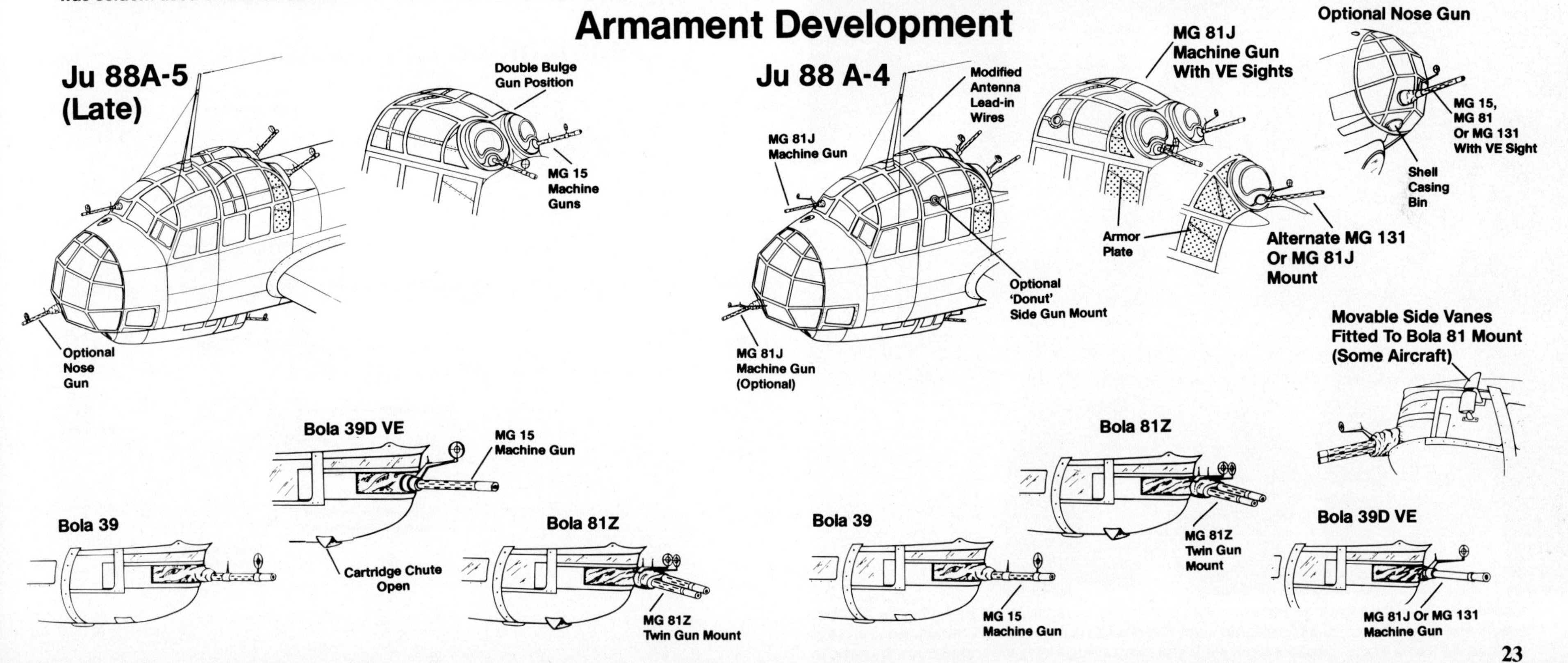

Collisions with Allied barrage balloons was one of the hazards faced by *Luftwaffe* bomber crews and a number of Ju 88A variants were fitted with an anti-balloon cable fender around the middle frame of the 'beetle's eye' nose. The reinforcing strips extended back along both sides of the fuselage below the cockpit.

A Ju 88A-4 of KG 3 carries colorful markings, the fuselage code (5K+FN) and propeller spinners are Red, the identification color of 5.*Staffel*, and the fusleage band is in Yellow. The windscreen machine gun is a belt fed MG 81. The gun's ammunition bin is visible through the upper nose glazing. KG3 was heavily committed to the Eastern Front.

Ammunition Bin Locations

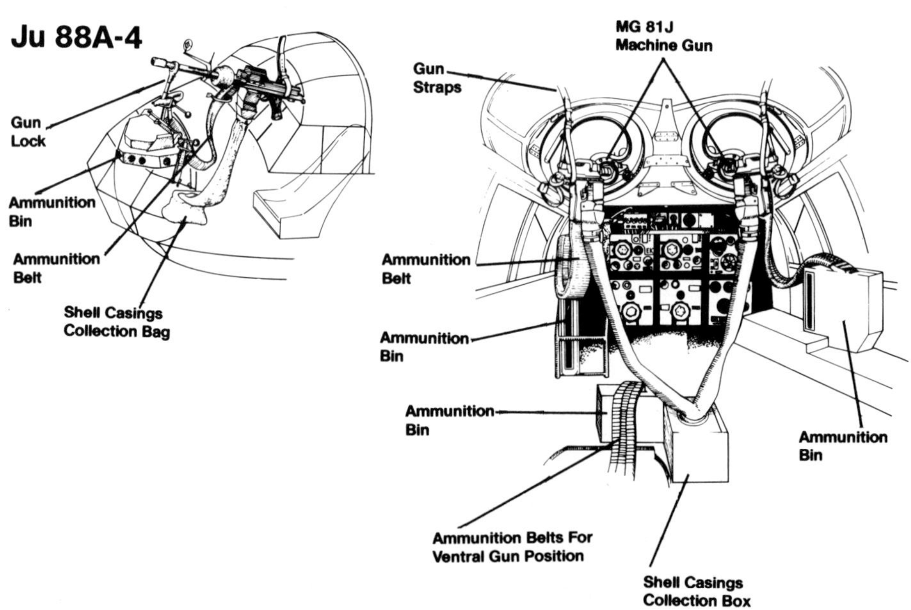

(Above) Ground crews push a bomb dolly toward a *Wellenmuster* (wave pattern) camouflaged Ju 88A-4 on an Italian airfield during late 1943. The *Wellenmuster* camouflage was used primarily for operations over water from mid-war onward.

(Below) The radio operator leaves the cockpit of a Ju 88A-4 following a crash landing which splintered the laminated wood of the port VS 11 propeller. The line running down the top of the fuselage is the tow line attached to the life raft which prevented the raft from drifting away after it was deployed. The pilot's fully armored seat is visible.

Nose Balloon Fender

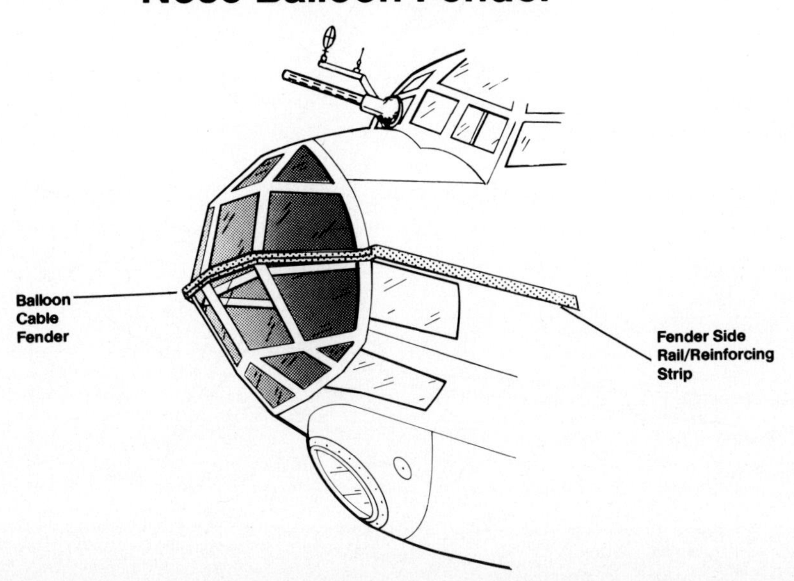

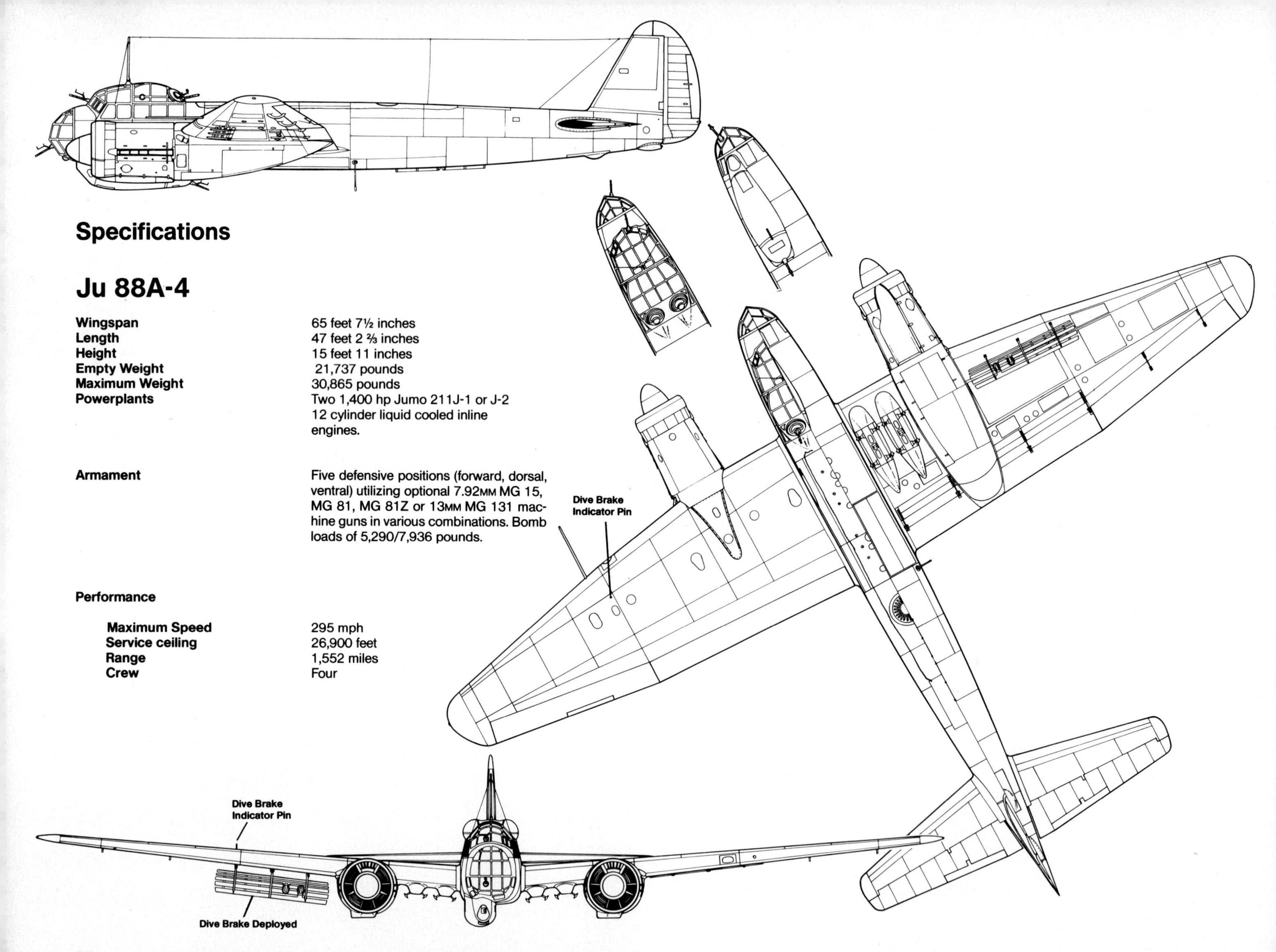

Specifications

Ju 88A-4

Wingspan	65 feet 7½ inches
Length	47 feet 2 ⅔ inches
Height	15 feet 11 inches
Empty Weight	21,737 pounds
Maximum Weight	30,865 pounds
Powerplants	Two 1,400 hp Jumo 211J-1 or J-2 12 cylinder liquid cooled inline engines.
Armament	Five defensive positions (forward, dorsal, ventral) utilizing optional 7.92MM MG 15, MG 81, MG 81Z or 13MM MG 131 machine guns in various combinations. Bomb loads of 5,290/7,936 pounds.
Performance	
Maximum Speed	295 mph
Service ceiling	26,900 feet
Range	1,552 miles
Crew	Four

(Above) The bright circles on the upper fuselage of these Ju 88A-4s is the EZ-6 direction finder cover. These semi-transparent plexiglass covers were lined with a 'starburst' pattern of metalized sensing strips on the inside of the cover. The two bright spots behind the EZ 6 covers are the antenna lead in points for the FuG 10 (front) and FuG 16 (rear) aerials.

(Below) A bomb fitted with a suspension block is maneuvered from a three wheeled bomb cart in preparation for loading on the inboard ETC rack of a Ju 88A-4. The tires used on the Ju 88A-4 were slightly larger than those used on earlier variants to handle the increased gross weight of the A-4, with the size increased from 1,100 x 375MM to 1,140 x 410MM.

Life Raft Compartment/EZ-6 Direction Finder

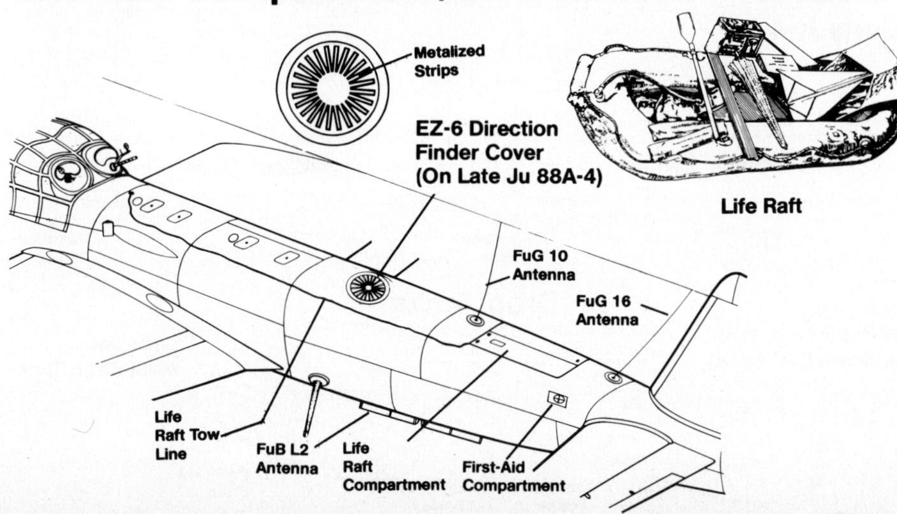

For long range missions or ferry flights several types of drop tanks or 'all purpose' containers could be carried on the ETC racks. This Ju 88A-4 carries a 900 liter (237 gallon) finned wooden fuel tank on the inboard rack. The empty tank could be dropped by pulling a release lever located in the radio operator's cockpit. (Feist)

The FuB1 2 blind landing approach radio antenna was comprised of six posts mounted on the underside of the fuselage to support the antenna wire. The Ju 88A-4 of 6./KG 3 in the background has the revised rudder introduced on mid-production Ju 88A-4s. The spinners, code letter 'B', fuselage band, and outline to the other code letters are in Yellow.

Rudder Development

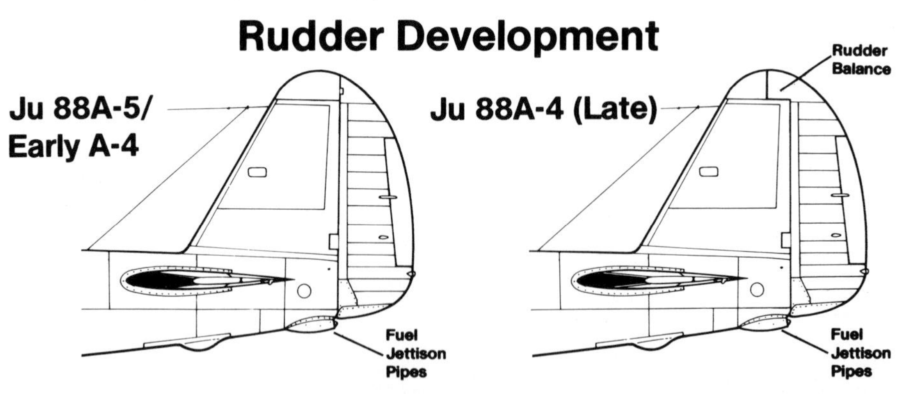

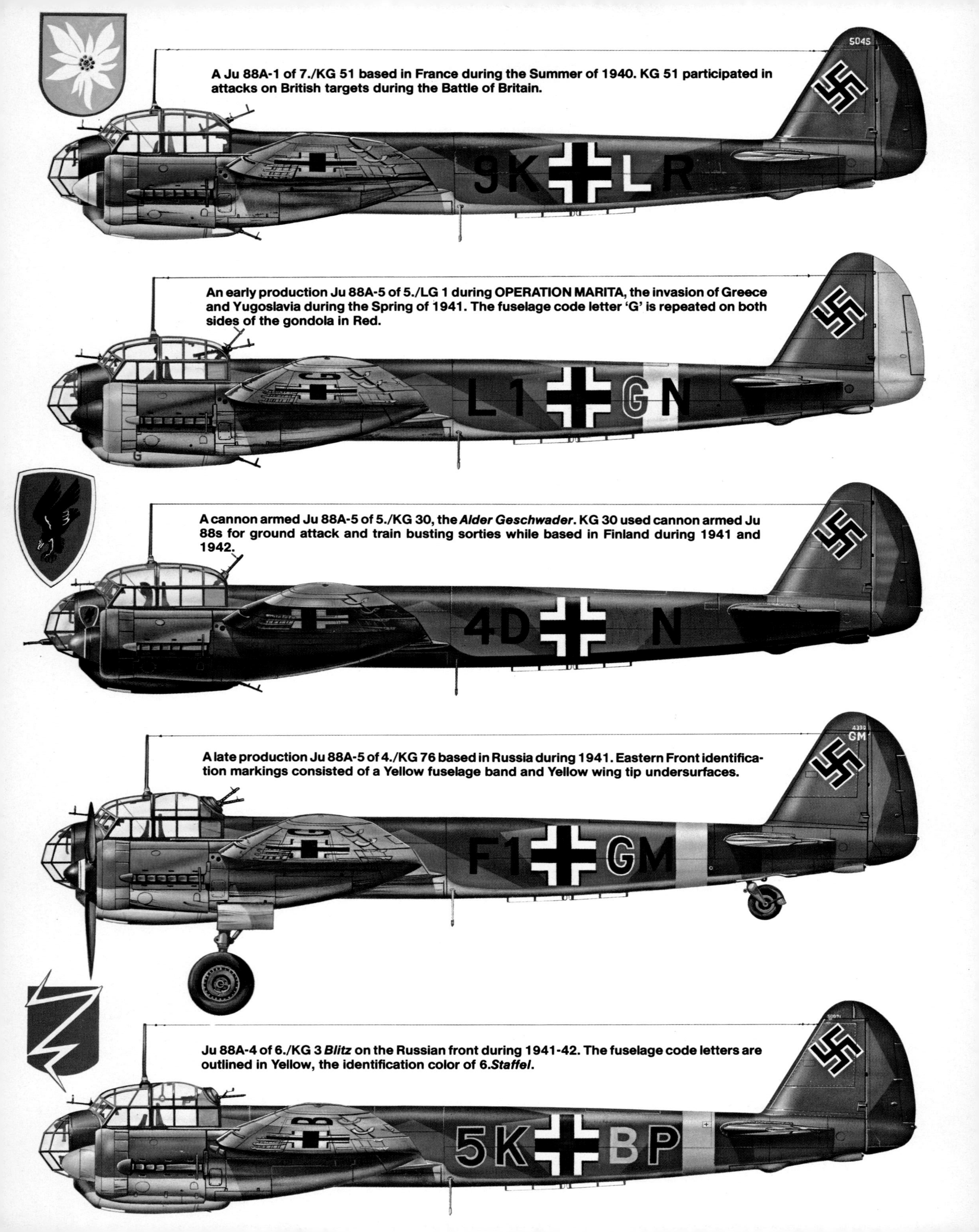

A Ju 88A-1 of 7./KG 51 based in France during the Summer of 1940. KG 51 participated in attacks on British targets during the Battle of Britain.

An early production Ju 88A-5 of 5./LG 1 during OPERATION MARITA, the invasion of Greece and Yugoslavia during the Spring of 1941. The fuselage code letter 'G' is repeated on both sides of the gondola in Red.

A cannon armed Ju 88A-5 of 5./KG 30, the *Alder Geschwader*. KG 30 used cannon armed Ju 88s for ground attack and train busting sorties while based in Finland during 1941 and 1942.

A late production Ju 88A-5 of 4./KG 76 based in Russia during 1941. Eastern Front identification markings consisted of a Yellow fuselage band and Yellow wing tip undersurfaces.

Ju 88A-4 of 6./KG 3 *Blitz* on the Russian front during 1941-42. The fuselage code letters are outlined in Yellow, the identification color of 6.*Staffel*.

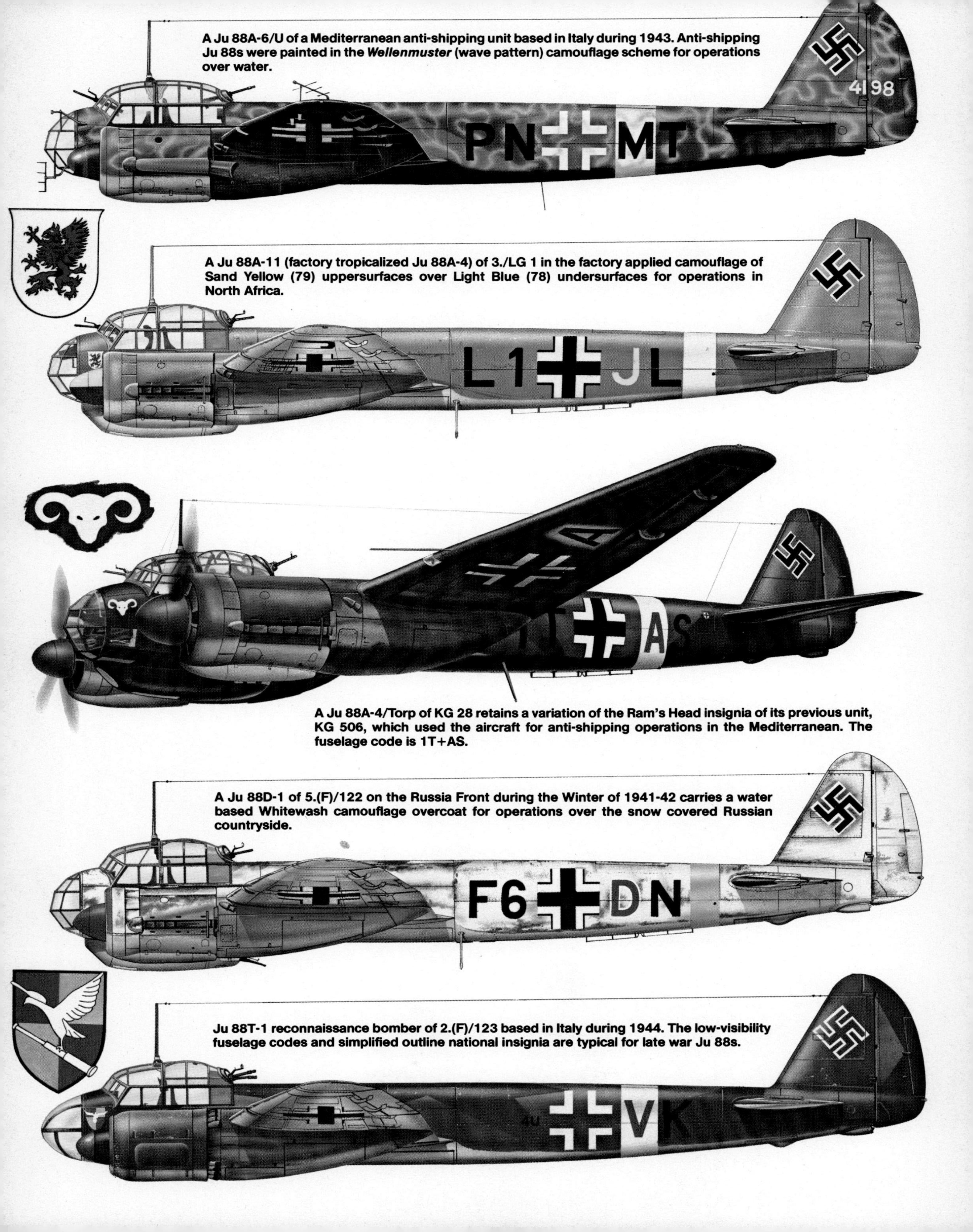

A Ju 88A-6/U of a Mediterranean anti-shipping unit based in Italy during 1943. Anti-shipping Ju 88s were painted in the *Wellenmuster* (wave pattern) camouflage scheme for operations over water.

A Ju 88A-11 (factory tropicalized Ju 88A-4) of 3./LG 1 in the factory applied camouflage of Sand Yellow (79) uppersurfaces over Light Blue (78) undersurfaces for operations in North Africa.

A Ju 88A-4/Torp of KG 28 retains a variation of the Ram's Head insignia of its previous unit, KG 506, which used the aircraft for anti-shipping operations in the Mediterranean. The fuselage code is 1T+AS.

A Ju 88D-1 of 5.(F)/122 on the Russia Front during the Winter of 1941-42 carries a water based Whitewash camouflage overcoat for operations over the snow covered Russian countryside.

Ju 88T-1 reconnaissance bomber of 2.(F)/123 based in Italy during 1944. The low-visibility fuselage codes and simplified outline national insignia are typical for late war Ju 88s.

A Ju 88A-4 of the *Fortelor Aeriene Regal ale Romana* (Royal Romanian Air Force) is refueled and rearmed for another mission on the Eastern Front. Ironically, these same Ju 88A-4s would later be used against German forces when an anti-axis coup took place in Romania during late 1943.

FuG 101 Radio Altimeter

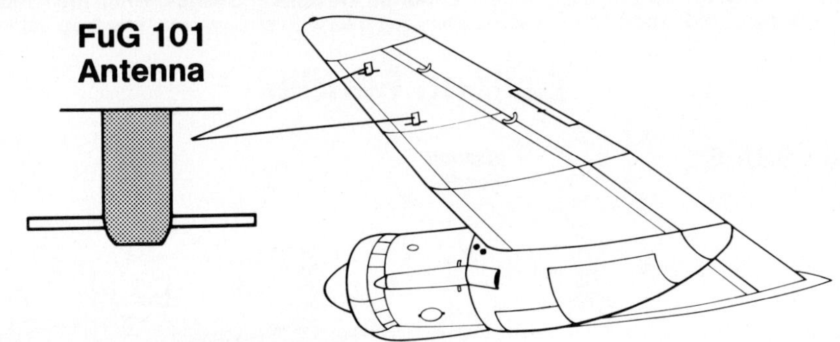

Pilot's Armored Seat

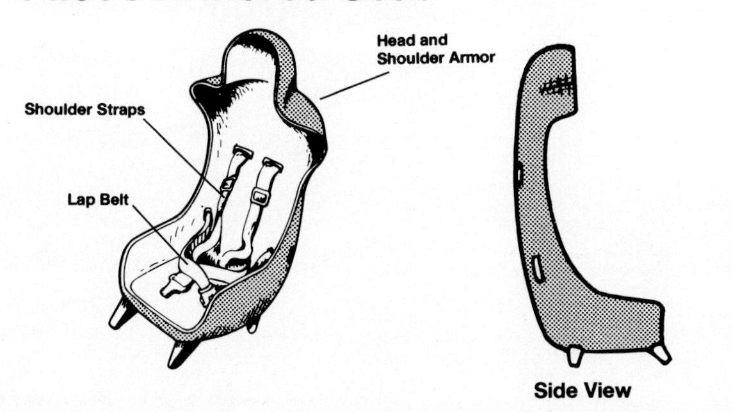

As one ground crewman checks the wing tanks of a Ju 88A-4, another tops off the auxilliary fuselage bomb-bay tank from the upper fuselage refueling point. Both bomb-bays could be equipped with fuel tanks, although the front bay was most commonly used for fuel. The rear bomb-bay four paneled doors are open ready to receive a bomb load once refueling is completed.

When a bomb was positioned the suspension block was locked into the rack opening, and the sway braces were tightened down against the bomb. When either fuselage bomb-bay was fitted with a four paneled door, the middle sections opened straight down from the fuselage centerline, while the outer doors opened down from the fuselage sides.

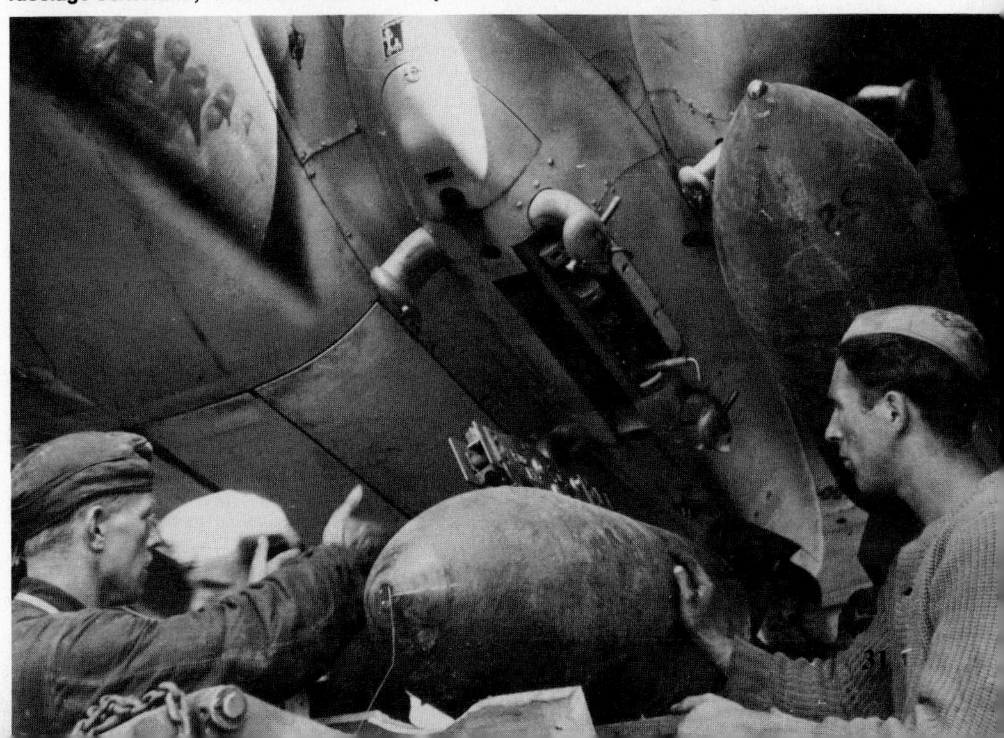

Ju 88A-6 and Ju 88A-6/U

The Ju 88A-6 designation was unique in that it eventually came to represent two very diverse aircraft, serving in two distinctly different roles. By the time the second, or Ju 88A-6/U variant had entered service, it bore little resemblance to its predecessor — the Ju 88A-6.

Ju 88A-6

During the early raids over England, collisions with British anti-aircraft barrage balloons had posed a serious and often fatal threat to bomber crews. The balloons were particularly effective at night when the balloons and their dangling cables were practically invisible. To counter this threat, both the He 111 and the Ju 88 were modified with specialized anti-balloon equipment.

During late 1940 a number of Ju 88A-5s were converted to the anti-balloon role with a large swept back cable fender mounted in front of the bomber supported by ten nose and wing leading edge struts under the designation Ju 88A-6. When the Ju 88A-6 flew into the cables strung below a barrage balloon, the cables would be deflected along the fenders to the wingtip, where they would be severed by cable cutters mounted on the wingtips. To offset the 840 pounds of the cable fender, a 130 pound counterweight was installed in the rear fuselage. Formations of Ju 88A-6s were to precede the main bomber force over the target to eliminate the balloon threat and allow the main force to attack the target at a lower altitude.

The weight and drag of the cable fender, however, cut the speed of the Ju 88A-6 by nearly 20 mph and severely impaired maneuverability making the aircraft vulnerable to enemy fighters and Flak. Although a number of operations were carried out by Ju 88A-6s during 1941, the system quickly proved impractical for wide spread use and after a few months of operations, most Ju 88A-6s had the fenders removed, reverting to the bomber role. The nose and wing fender attachment brackets were usually retained and covered with streamlined 'tear drop' fairings. One Ju 88 A-6 (coded 4D+DL, Werk-Nr. 3457) was examined by the British when it crash landed in England on 27 July 1941. In the official British intelligence report the bomber was described simply as being *"...like the Ju 88A-5 but with balloon fenders..."*.

Ju 88A-6/U

With the failure of the anti-balloon Ju 88A-6, these aircraft were gradually returned to factory conversion centers for conversion to anti-shipping bombers under the designation Ju 88A-6/U. The balloon fender attachments were removed and the aircraft updated with Jumo 211F or J engines bringing them up to Ju 88A-4 standards (a number of Ju 88A-6/Us are believed to have been built directly from Ju 88A-4 airframes). The ventral gondola was removed (reducing the crew to three), being replaced with a simple belly crew entry hatch. An FuG 200 *Hohentwiel* search radar with yagi antennas was mounted on three masts attached to the extreme nose. The FuG 200 radar was often augmented with a *Rostock* or FuG 217 radar, both of which featured wing mounted antenna arrays.

A number of Ju 88A-6/Us had one FuG 200 antenna mast mounted on the nose with the remaining antennas mounted one on each wing leading edge just outboard of the engine nacelle. Once in service, additional changes were made in the field, including extended flame dampening exhaust shrouds and varying standards of defensive armament. A number of Ju 88A-6/Us carried a single MG 81 or 13MM MG 131 rear canopy gun mount, others carried twin bulged rear canopy MG 81 mounts. In addition a small number of Ju 88A-6/Us carried an MG 81 gun mounted in the starboard windshield position to increase forward firepower.

Ju 88A-6/U's remained in service throughout the war, flying from bases in France, Norway, and Italy in a maritime reconnaissance and anti-shipping role. Occasionally these bombers were used to 'shadow' Allied bomber formations with their radar. The FuG 200 radar could detect surface vessels at a range of up to 50 miles, while the FuG 217 could be used as both a forward looking or tail warning radar. The use of alternate radars offset any deficiencies between the radars and allowed for more complete coverage of the search area.

The Ju 88A-6 was identical to the Ju 88A-5 with the exception of the brackets for mounting the anti-barrage balloon cable fender/cutter on the nose and wings. When the fender was not in place the brackets were sometimes covered with streamlined 'teardrop' fairings.

Balloon Fender

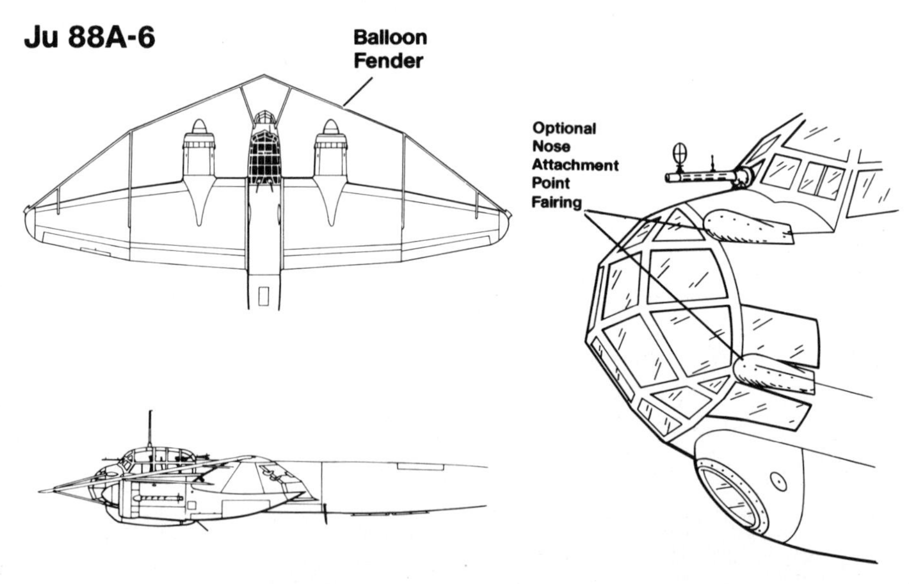

F1+GS, a Ju 88A-6 of 8./KG 76 returns to base after a night mission. The balloon fender attachment brackets are just visible on the nose in front of the cockpit. The thin band around the fuselage behind the wing and outline of the fuselage letter 'G' are Red, while the letters 'GS' and Swastika on the fin have been overpainted in Black.

A number of Ju 88A-6 airframes were rebuilt and modified for the anti-shipping role under the designation Ju 88A-6/U. This Ju 88A-6/U has had FuG 200 radar antennas installed on the nose, and the windscreen machine gun position covered with a metal plug .These FuG 200 masts are fixed non-pivoting types.

Radar Installation

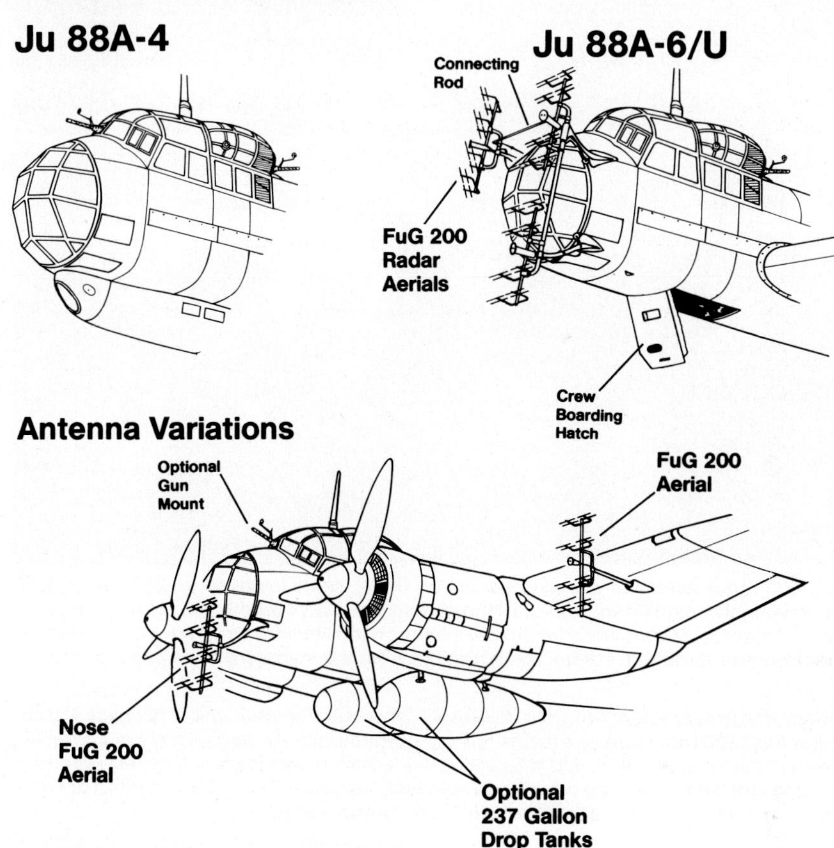

Armament Variations

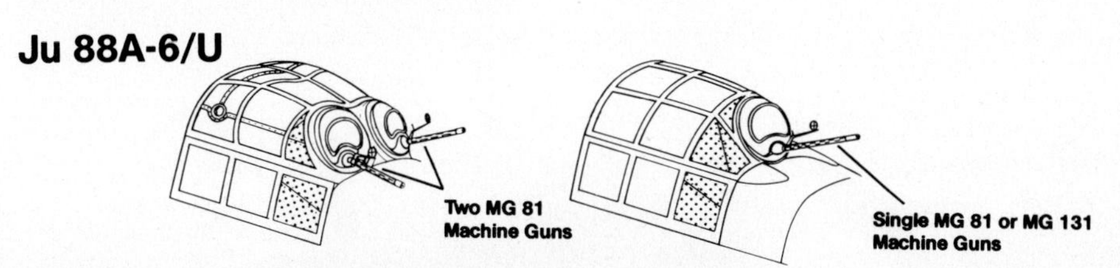

Optional Extended Exhaust Shroud

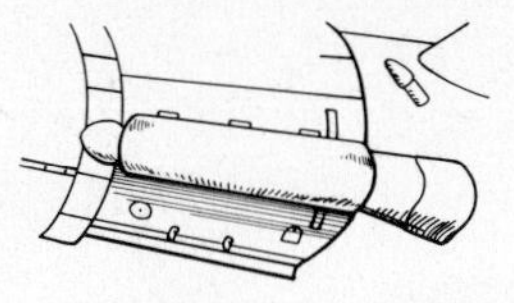

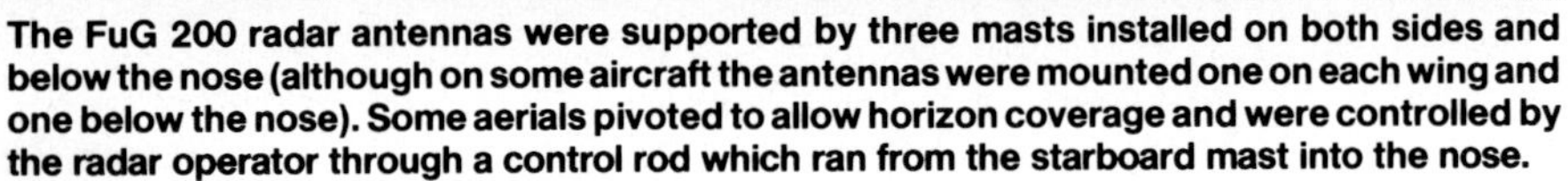

The FuG 200 radar antennas were supported by three masts installed on both sides and below the nose (although on some aircraft the antennas were mounted one on each wing and one below the nose). Some aerials pivoted to allow horizon coverage and were controlled by the radar operator through a control rod which ran from the starboard mast into the nose.

Crew members prepare to board their Ju 88A-6/U through the open under fuselage-hatch. The upper FuG 200 radar antenna masts are in place although the aerials have not been fitted. A recent conversion, this A-6/U still retains the factory fuselage code (PN+MT) used for test and delivery flights. The uppersurfaces are camouflaged with an RLM Gray (02) or Light Blue (76) wave pattern over Dark Green with Black undersurfaces.

A Ju 88A-6/U equipped with outer wing radar antennas (either the FuG 217 or a derivative of the *Rostock* radar system). The use of different radars allowed more complete coverage of the search area. The 'T' shaped antenna under the wing is the FuG 101 radio altimeter antenna, common on all later Ju 88A variants.

Optional Wing Radar Installations

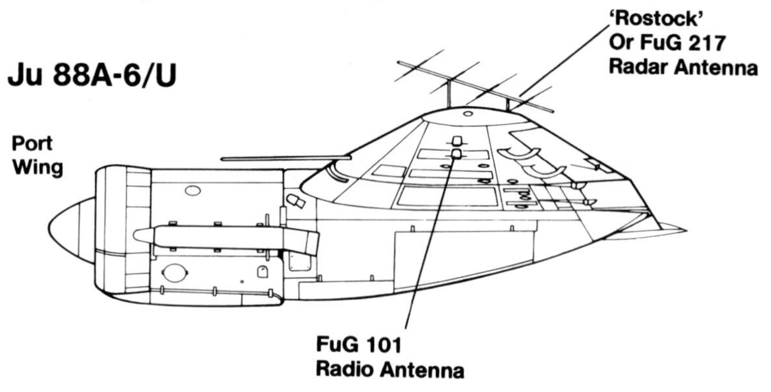

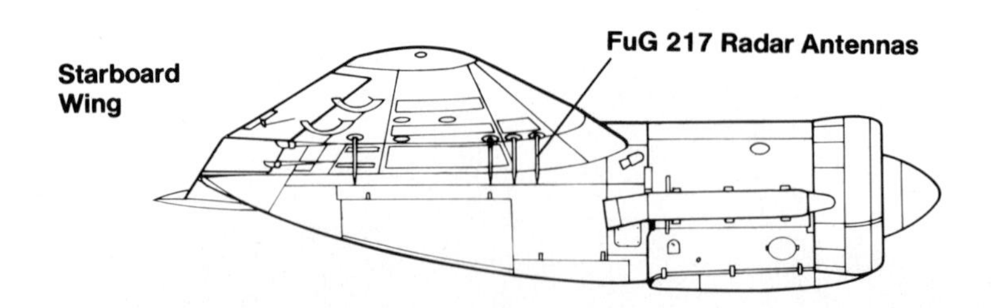

Ju 88A-7

The Ju 88A-7 was an unarmed dual control trainer variant of the Ju 88A-5 incorporating the long span wing and powered by 1,200 hp Jumo 211H-1 engines. A number of Ju 88A-7s also had the gondola removed.

Ju 88A-8

The Ju 88A-8 was based on the Ju 88A-4 airframe modified to accept the anti-balloon cable fenders of the Ju 88A-6. Although a number of early machines were fitted with the attachment points, the cable fender itself had proven to be impractical and it is believed that none were actually installed. Instead, the remaining Ju 88A-8s produced are believed to have been fitted with full span wing leading edge cable cutters.

The wing leading edge cable cutters, known as *Kuto-Nase* cutters, were designed to sever any cables which came in contact with the wing leading edge. Encased under a thin outer skin of collapsible metal (such as tin) the cutters ran along the wing leading edge from just outboard of the engine nacelle to a point just inboard of the wing tip. While production of the Ju 88A-8 was limited, the *Kuto-Nase* cutters proved successful, being utilized on later Ju 88A variants and other *Luftwaffe* bombers.

Tropical Ju 88s: Ju 88A-9, A-10 and A-11

When the *Luftwaffe* began operations in North Africa and the Mediterranean, it quickly became obvious that its aircraft would require specialized desert equipment. Desert modifications for the Ju 88 included the addition of internal sand filters on the engine air intakes and desert survival gear for the crew — additional water containers, sun-shades and weapons for hunting. Externally, these modifications did little to alter the appearance of the Ju 88A-1, A-4 or A-5 aircraft which were retro-fitted with desert equipment under the designation *Tropisch* (Tropical).

Aircraft modified at conversion centers were designated Ju 88A-1/Trop, A-4/Trop and A-5/Trop. The introduction of desert equipment to Ju 88s on the production line resulted in three additional sub-types: Ju 88A-9 (tropical version of the Ju 88A-1), Ju 88A-10 (tropical version of the Ju 88A-5), and Ju 88A-11 (tropical version of the Ju 88A-4). The Ju 88A-5/Trop and Ju 88A-10 along with the Ju 88A-4/Trop and Ju 88A-11 were the most widely used and saw considerable action in the Mediterranean and North Africa. Few, if any, Ju 88A-1/Trop or Ju 88A-9s were actually committed to combat. With the surrender of Axis forces in the desert during the spring of 1943, the surviving tropicalized Ju 88s were transferred to units in Italy.

Kuto-Nase Cable Cutter

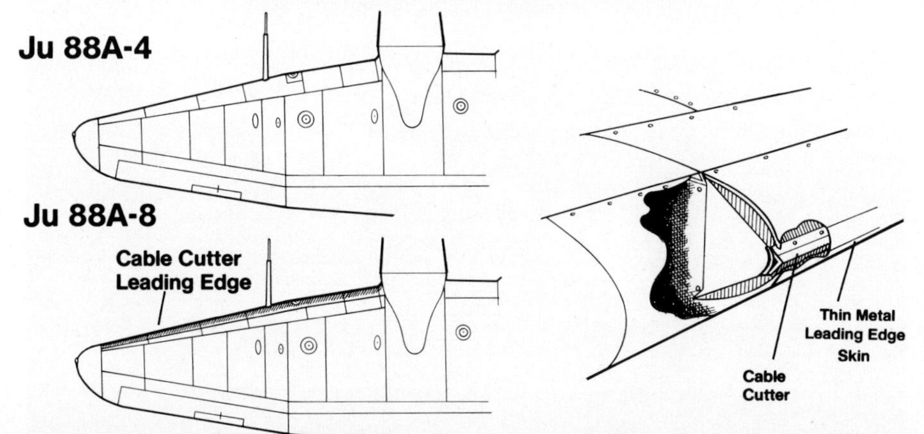

A number of Ju 88A-4 airframes were modified with anti-barrage balloon fenders under the designation Ju 88A-8. It is unclear if the fenders were ever actually used, however, a number of aircraft had the attachment points in place and covered with 'teardrop' fairings. In the event use of the balloon fender was abandoned and the Ju 88A-8 was fitted with *Kuto-Nase* wing leading edge cable cutters.

Ju 88A-12

The Ju 88A-12 was a trainer variant of the Ju 88A-4 with a slightly widened cockpit for improved crew accommodation. In common with the earlier Ju 88A-3 and A-7, the Ju 88A-12 carried duplicate controls for both the instructor and student. Equipment not needed for the training role such as the dive brakes, armament, and ventral gondola, were removed. Ju 88A-12s were conversions from existing Ju 88A-4 airframes carried out at specialized conversion centers.

This desert camoufaged Ju 88A-5/Trop of LG 1 has been cannibalized for parts after a crash landing in North Africa. The guns, life raft, engine components, and wing tip navigation lights have been removed for use on other Ju 88s. The Ju 88A-5/Trop designation indicated an aircraft converted for desert operations at a conversion center. Some components of this aircraft retain their original Dark Green European camouflage.

A Ju 88A-10 (L1+LW) of 12./LG 1 parked on a North African airfield has the canopy shielded by a tarp. The bomber carries both a White and Yellow fuselage band. The fuselage code letter 'L' is in Yellow, the identification color of 12.*Staffel*. Ju 88A-10s were factory tropicalized variants of the Ju 88A-5. The designation 'Trop' is applied under the *Werk-Nummer* on the fin tip in White.

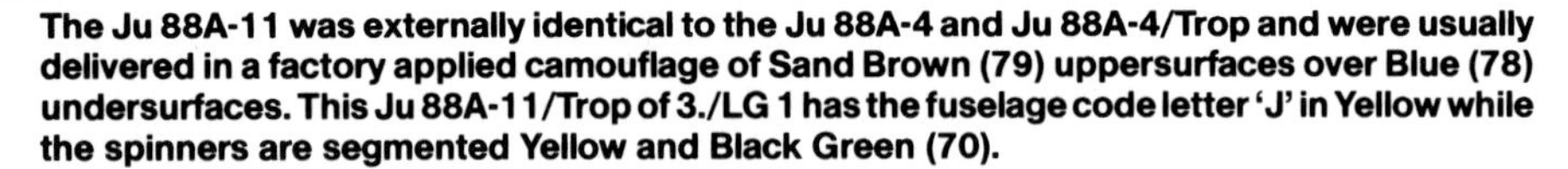

The Ju 88A-11 was externally identical to the Ju 88A-4 and Ju 88A-4/Trop and were usually delivered in a factory applied camouflage of Sand Brown (79) uppersurfaces over Blue (78) undersurfaces. This Ju 88A-11/Trop of 3./LG 1 has the fuselage code letter 'J' in Yellow while the spinners are segmented Yellow and Black Green (70).

A Ju 88A-11 (L1+OK) returns from a mission with the port propeller feathered. The bomber carries a field applied mottle of Green (80) over the factory applied Sand Brown (79) uppersurface camouflage.

Ju 88A-13

The Ju 88A-13 was developed for the ground attack role with particular emphasis on anti-personnel operations. According to an Allied intelligence report of 7 April 1942, the original official German description of the Ju 88A-13 was as follows:

> "... As Ju 88 A-1, only Condition A; SD-2 Bomb installation; extra armor; MG/FF 20mm cannon in 'A' nose position, however, without Lotfe BZG 2 bombsight and without dive brakes and automatic pull out device... '.

Eventually the Ju 88A-13, which reportedly made its first appearance in January of 1942, became a limited production aircraft based on the Ju 88A-4 airframe incorporating additional armor protection for the lower cockpit, fuel tanks, and undersides of the engine nacelles with the dive brakes and associated equipment being removed. Along with its internal bomb load, the Ju 88A-13 could be armed with *Abwurfbehälter* (droppable holders) AB 250, AB 500 and AB 1000 containers capable of carrying weapons such as the 4.4 pound SD-2 'butterfly' anti-personnel bomblet.

For strafing enemy troop concentrations, the Ju 88A-13 could also carry the *Waffenbehälter* (weapons holders) WB 81A or B gun pods. These self contained gun pods carried up to three 7.9MM MG 81Z twin machine guns along with their ammunition trays. The pods differed only in the angle of inclination of the guns, either 0 or 15 degrees. With four pods mounted on the ETC racks the Ju 88A-13 was a formidable ground strafer. It is believed that the majority of Ju 88A-13s were used on the Eastern Front where their firepower could be used with devastating effect against Soviet troops.

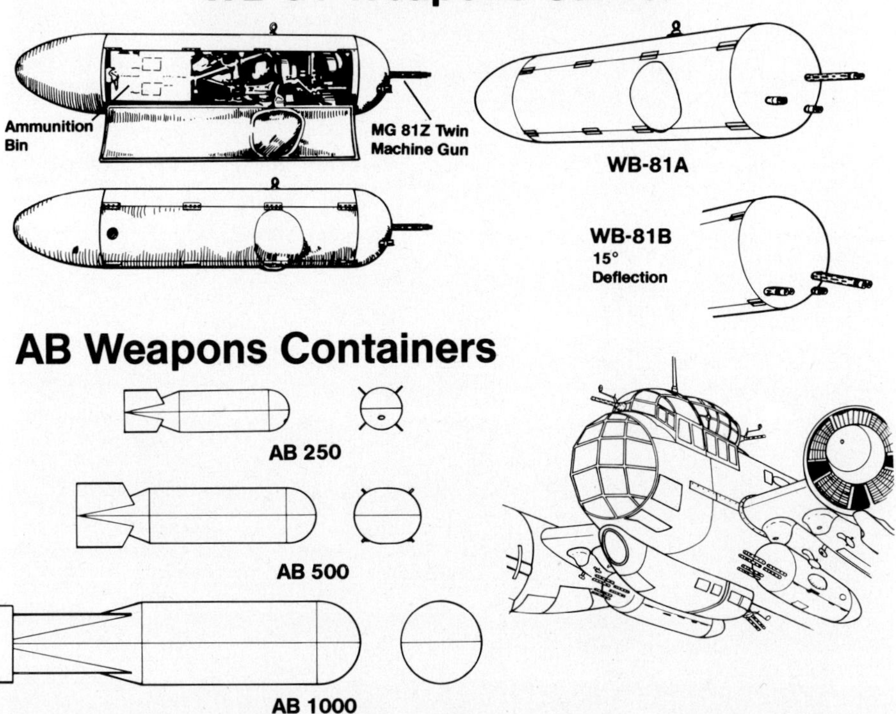

Cannon Armed Ju 88s

In an effort to improve the Ju 88's forward firepower conversion kits known as *Änderungsmaterial* (alteration material), were designed which allowed a fixed Oerlikon MG/FF 20MM cannon to be installed in the starboard side of the nose. The lower glass panel on the starboard side of the nose was replaced with a concave panel reinforced to hold the cannon barrel. The Lotfe bombsight was removed and the bomb sight glass panel either faired over or simply over painted. The MG/FF cannon fired at a rate of 520 rounds per minute and the 120 round ammunition drums were manually changed in flight by the bombardier. The nose mounted cannon conversion kit could be installed on practically any variant of the Ju 88A.

The increase in forward firepower offered by the MG/FF conversion proved extremely popular with operational units, with cannon armed Ju 88s serving alongside standard bomber variants in KG 51, KG 54, KG 76, as well as various *Aufklärungsgruppen* (Reconnaissance Groups) and anti-shipping units. *Lehrgeschwader 1* utilized a number of cannon armed Ju 88s in the Mediterranean and North Africa, both for anti-shipping and anti-armor missions, while KG 30 used its cannon armed Ju 88A-4s and A-5s for train busting sorties along the Murmansk railway from bases in Finland.

The success of the nose mounted cannon conversion led to a factory re-design for mounting the cannon in the ventral gondola. The re-design consisted of replacing the bomb sight's oval shaped optical glass panel with a shorter flat topped panel. The rounded nose of the gondola was cut back and a flat end plate installed. Whenever a cannon was field installed the flat end plate was removed with the cannon barrel protruded from the opening. Since the bomb sight was removed during the conversion, the optical panel was often overpainted or faired over from the inside. Optional accessories for the cannon included muzzle flash hiders and a ring-and-bead sight mounted on a tall rod attached to the barrel.

In a effort to increase forward firepower a 20MM MG/FF cannon was mounted in the nose of the Ju 88. These field conversions consisted of removing the bomb sight and installing a cannon in the bombardier's position with the cannon protruding from a concave glass panel. This cannon armed Ju 88 of 1.(F)/120 has the bomb sight window overpainted in Light Blue.

Ju 88A-14

The popularity of these cannon conversions led to production of a standardized cannon armed attack bomber under the designation Ju 88A-14. The Ju 88A-14 was essentially a strengthened Ju 88A-4 airframe, modified for low level attack and anti-shipping roles. *Kuto-Nase* leading edge cable cutters and additional interior armor plate became standard with the underwing dive brakes being eliminated. The MG/FF cannon was added to some Ju 88A-14s in a factory built ventral gondola position which differed from the conversion kit mountings in having a solid 'mantle' at the base of the cannon barrel and a shell ejection chute installed on the faired over the bomb sight panel.

With the ETC bomb racks retained, the Ju 88A-14 could carry a formidable array of weapons. One A-14 (Werk-Nr. 140286), believed to be coded 3Z+YR, crashed at Sidi Makrelouf on 22 March 1943. Allied personnel who examined the aircraft found that this Ju 88A-14 carried an unusual armament of sixteen small ETC 50/VIII bomb racks each capable of carrying a single 50 kg (110 lb) bomb in place of the standard ETC underwing bomb racks.

Without the cannon installation, the Ju 88A-14 was externally identical to the Ju 88A-4, possessing similar defensive armament. The weight of the cannon and extra armor, however, did decrease performance somewhat.

(Right) Pilots of LG 1 exchange cigarettes in front of a cannon armed Ju 88A-4. The side armor plating inside the 'beetle's-eye' nose was common on cannon armed Ju 88s and some standard bombers. The small side windows on the fuselage were often covered with armor as well, providing the crew with extra armor protection during low level missions.

(Bottom) A cannon armed Ju 88A-4 of KG 76 has the bomb sight window faired over from within which allowed the bomb sight to be reinstalled later if needed. The ETC bomb racks were often retained on cannon armed Ju 88s for low level bombing.

(Above) A cannon armed Ju 88A-4 of II/KG 51 makes its approach for landing at an airfield on the Russian front. The barrel of the gondola mounted MG/FF cannon carries a flash arrester to prevent the muzzle flash from blinding the aircrew during night operations.

(Right) This cannon armed Ju 88A-4 has the MG/FF cannon mounted in the ventral gondola with a post mounted ring-and-bead fixed to the cannon barrel. When carried in the gondola the ammunition drum of the MG/FF cannon projected into the cockpit through an opening in the floor board, allowing the bombardier to change drums in flight.

(Above) A late production Ju 88A-5 of II/KG 30 has the windscreen MG 15 removed, an anti-balloon nose fender installed, and an MG/FF 20MM cannon mounted in the nose. The White circular shape inside the nose is the 120 round ammunition drum for the MG/FF cannon.

Some limited production Ju 88A-14s had the 20MM cannon factory installed in the gondola. The bombsight window was faired over and equipped with a shell ejection chute, while the front of the gondola was reinforced at the base of the cannon barrel. Ju 88A-14s were used for both anti-shipping and low level ground assault.

The factory installed flat faced gondola cannon mounting enabled late production Ju 88A-4s and Ju 88A-14s to be easily converted to the cannon armed configuration. This Italian based (either a late Ju 88A-4 or Ju 88A-14) carries the flat faced gondola and cropped bomb sight window with the bomb sight in place.

Cannon Installation

Field Conversion Ju 88A

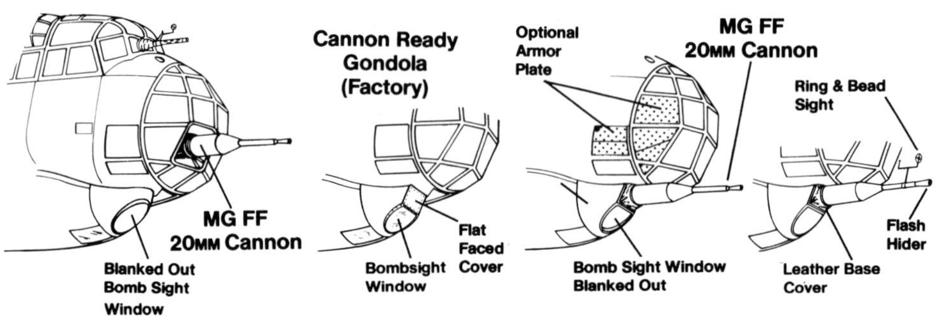

Ju 88 A-14
(Factory Mount)

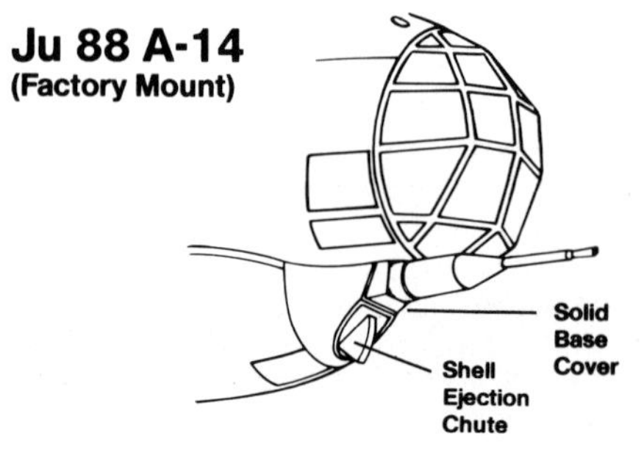

Ju 88A-15

The Ju 88A-15 was a development of the Ju 88A-4 which attempted to accommodate the bombers full bomb load internally, eliminating the drag producing external under wing racks. A large wooden bomb-bay with folding bomb-bay doors, was mounted under the fuselage extending over both the front and rear internal bomb-bays. This enlarged bomb-bay was capable of carrying 6,614 pounds of bombs, just 1,300 pounds under the maximum load of the Ju 88A-4. The underwing bomb racks and ventral gondola were removed and a streamlined fairing was added under the nose for the bombsight periscope.

Defensive armament was restricted to the upper rear canopy and windscreen machine gun mounts which were fitted with either MG 15 or MG 81 machine guns. A number of references suggest that fixed rear firing MG 17 machine guns were added to the rear of the wooden bomb-bay fairing to compensate the loss of the ventral gondola gun position.

The Ju 88A-15 offered little improvement in performance over the Ju 88 variants already in service and production was limited to a small number of aircraft.

Equipped with a research boom on its starboard wing, this Ju 88A-15 (Werk-Nr. 140561) was retained by Junkers for test trials. The huge wooden under fuselage bomb-bay carried the bomb load internally, eliminating the ETC under wing bomb racks. A steamlined fairing under the nose housed the bomb sight. (Gene Stafford)

Ju 88A-16

The Ju 88A-16 was a dual control trainer variant, widely reported as a trainer version of the Ju 88A-14. At least one source, however, states that the A-16 was a training variant of the Ju 88A-15 produced to train pilots on the different flight characteristics produced by the Ju 88A-15's large under fuselage bomb-bay. In either case, the Ju 88A-16 was similar to other trainer variants with flight controls installed for both the instructor and student and having the ventral gondola and armament removed.

Carrying a pair of torpedos, a Ju 88A-4/Torp prepares for take-off with the aid of Walter rocket pods carried under each outboard wing. The bulged fairing for the torpedo control lines was on the starboard side of the nose only.

Ju 88A-4/Torp

The *Luftwaffe* lacked a dedicated torpedo bomber and was forced to modify other aircraft, such as the Ju 88 and Heinkel He 111 to serve in the torpedo bomber role. Conversion kits were produced in early 1942 to modify the Ju 88A-4 to carry two 1,686 pound LT F5b or similarly sized torpedos on enlarged underwing racks under the designation Ju 88A-4/Torp (torpedo). The conversion consisted of removing the dive brakes, automatic pullout equipment, and ETC bomb racks and installing a PVC torpedo rack under each wing root. The PVC torpedo racks were larger and deeper than the ETC bomb racks and featured a different shackle arrangement. To allow for steering adjustments to the torpedos prior to release, a slender bulged fairing (which housed the torpedo controls) was added along the starboard side of the fuselage connecting the bombardier's station with the PVC racks.

Other than the specialized torpedo equipment, the Ju 88A-4/Torp differed little from the standard Ju 88A-4. The defensive armament positions remained unchanged, and a variety of optional equipment could be carried including FuG 101 radio altimeter, FuG 200 search radar, nose or gondola mounted MG/FF cannon, exhaust shrouds, nose mounted cable fenders, and Walter rocket pods.

One experimental installation involved the use of two 'glider torpedos' carried on special wing racks mounted under the outer wing panels on a Ju 88A-4 (BF+YT, Werk Nr 740). The 'glider torpedo' was a combination of a standard torpedo with a Blohm & Voss L10 glider. The glider's nine foot wings allowed the bomber to release the torpedo from higher altitudes. After release the glide torpedo would glide into the water at a 15 degree angle. Upon impact with the water, the glider's wings and tail would break free from the torpedo. The glide torpedo project was abandoned shortly after BF+YT suffered a landing gear collapse while undergoing tests at Gotenhafen.

Ju 88A-17

The success of the Ju 88A-4/Torp led to a decision to produce a limited number of production aircraft based on the Ju 88A-4 and A-14 airframes under the designation Ju 88A-17. The Ju 88A-17 differed primarily from the earlier converted aircraft in having the ventral gondola deleted. The torpedo combat load was identical to the earlier Ju 88A-4/Torp and the same optional equipment carried on the A-4/Torp could be fitted to the A-17.

Both the Ju 88A-4/Torp and Ju 88A-17 served in the same theaters and in many of the same units. At varying periods; KG 26, KG 28, KG 76, KG 77 and *Kampfgruppe* 506 (K.Gr. 506) are known to have operated both variants in the anti-shipping role.

(Above) This Ju 88A-4/Torp (A8+CM) is believed to be assigned to the experimental 4.*(Versuchs) Staffel*/KSG 2 in Italy. The Ju 88A-4/Torp was the initial torpedo bomber variant field converted using factory supplied conversion kits.

(Below) A Ju 88A-4/Torp pulls up after releasing its torpedo. The low altitudes required for torpedo attacks made the bombers vunerable to anti-aircraft fire from the ships they were attacking. The Heinkel He 111, Ju 88A-4/Torp and Ju 88A-17 were the best torpedo bombers available to the *Luftwaffe*.

Torpedo Bomber Development

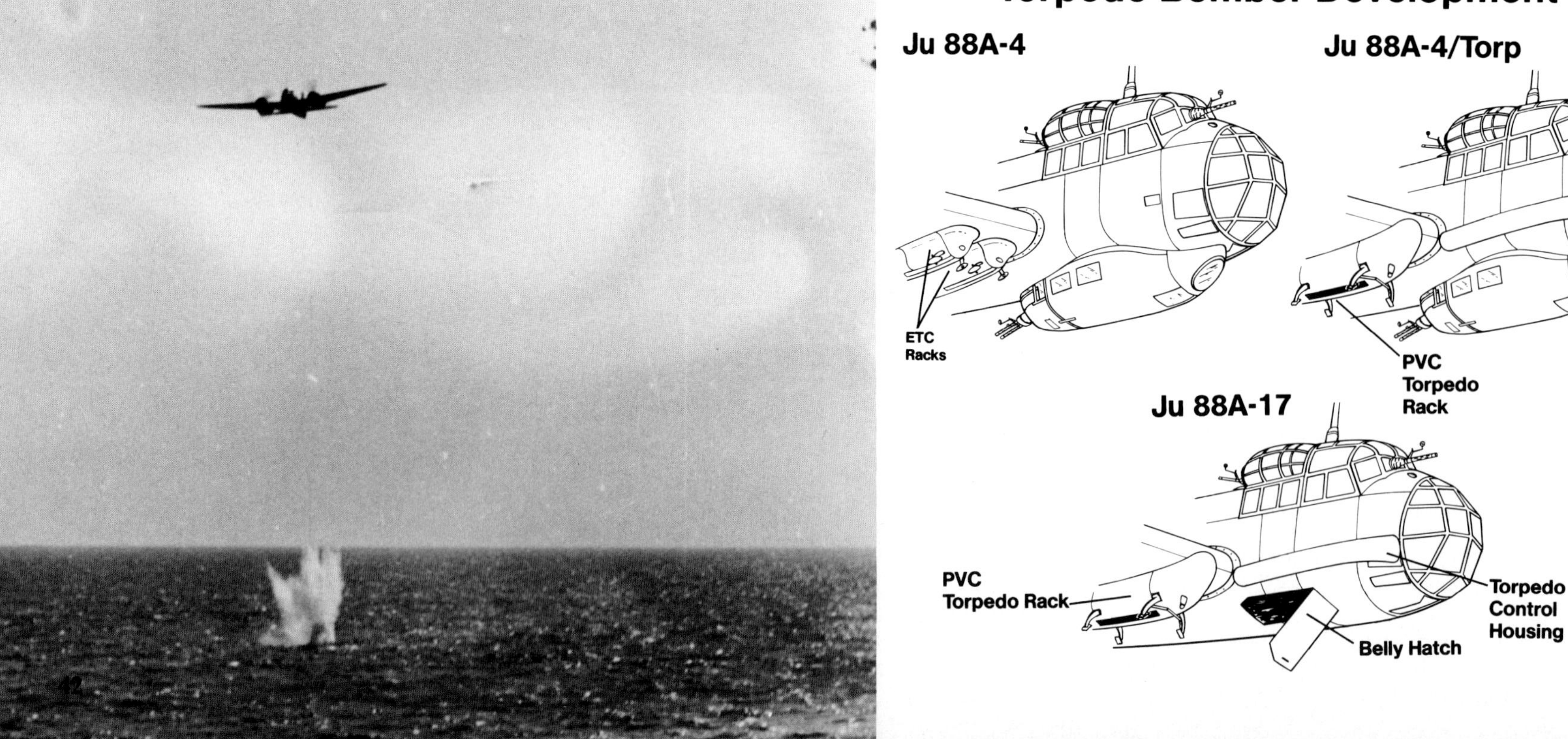

The Red and White striped warhead indicates that this is a practice torpedo being loading on the port rack of a Ju 88A-4/Torp. Just visible on the side of the nose is the 'Ram's head' unit shield originally of K.Gr. 506. The undersurfaces have been painted Black, however, the lower front of the cowlings remain in the the original Light Blue (65).

Ju 88A-17s of KG 26 prepare for a torpedo strike from their base at Bardufoss, Norway. The lead aircraft is believed to be a Ju 88A-17 fitted with FuG 200 *Hohentwiel* surface search radar for target location. The limited production Ju 88A-17 had the ventral gondola deleted to reduce both drag and weight.

(Above and Below) Groundcrewmen raise a 1,686 pound LT F5b torpedo into position under the PVC torpedo rack on a Ju 88A-4/Torp. PVC racks were larger and deeper than the ETC bomb rack, and featured a different shackle arrangement. The oversized wooden fins on the torpedo stabilized it after release and broke off upon impact with the water. The Ju 88A-4/Torp and Ju 88A-17 could carry two such weapons.

Ju 88B

During the original design work on the Ju 85 and Ju 88 in 1936, two alternative variants (designated Ju 85B and Ju 88B) were proposed, both designs featuring a bullet shaped 'bubble' canopy which would reduce drag and improve forward vision. Although a full scale cabin mock-up for the Ju 85B was completed, the entire plan was dismissed as too unconventional by the *Technisches Amt* of the RLM and shelved.

The Junkers design team re-submitted the 'unconventional' concept three years later, basing their updated design on the Ju 88A-1 airframe with the prototype 1,500 hp Jumo 213 engine as the power plant. The new forward fuselage incorporated a curved glazed canopy extending from the nose over the top of the cockpit ending in a smoothly faired-in rear gun position. Interior crew seating was similar to that of a standard Ju 88A. To house the bombardier's Lotfe bombsight periscope, a tear drop shaped external fairing was mounted under the starboard side of the nose. The lower fuselage was bulged to make room for a rear firing ventral gun position. The RLM, however, was pleased with the progress of the Ju 88A, considering its performance adequate for the *Luftwaffe's* needs. Junkers was granted permission to proceed with the Ju 88B program, but only on a low priority basis.

Throughout 1940 Junkers continued development of the Ju 88B. Since the in-line Jumo 213 engine was still in the development phase, Junker's decided to use the 1,600 hp BMW 801MA twin row, fourteen cylinder radial engine to power the prototypes. Three prototypes were built including the Ju 88 V-23 bomber variant, the Ju 88 V-24 reconnaissance variant, and the Ju 88 V-25 *Zerstörer* (destroyer) variant with a forward battery of three 7.9MM MG 17s and one MG 151 20MM, mounted on the starboard side of the nose. The prototypes made their first flights in July (Ju 88B V-23), September (Ju 88B V-24) and October (Ju 88B V-25) of 1940. It was intended that the pototypes would be followed by production aircraft under the designations Ju 88B-1 (bomber), B-2 (reconnaissance), and B-3 (destroyer).

The first prototype was based on the Ju 88A-1 airframe but featured the extended wings of the Ju 88A-5. The underwing ETC bomb racks were augmented by installation of an additional ETC bomb rack mounted outboard of each engine nacelle. Tests with an early prototype D-AUVS (also referred to as the Ju 88B V-1), revealed an increased level of performance slightly superior to that of the Ju 88A-1. The RLM, however, did not consider this improvement in performance sufficient to warrant disruption of Ju 88A production.

As a result, only ten pre-production Ju 88B-0s were authorized. These aircraft were based on the Ju 88A-4 airframe, featuring a lengthened forward fuselage to improve stability (extending overall length to approximately 49 feet). The majority of the Ju 88B-0 airframes were modified for the reconnaissance role with the bomb sight, outer wing bomb racks, and dive brakes being deleted. The fuselage bomb-bays were faired over with a large fuel tank being installed in the space normally used for the front bomb-bay. A battery of three cameras were mounted in the rear bomb-bay area with two camera windows installed on the starboard side of the fuselage undersides and a third window on the port side.

Armament consisted of three flexible MG 81Z machine guns mounted in the ventral, windscreen, and dorsal positions. The Ju 88B-0 had a top speed between 311 and 335 mph, service ceiling of 30,840 feet, and a range of 1,769 miles. A number of these aircraft were assigned to the *Aufklärungsgruppe des Oberbefehlshabers der Luftwaffe* (Reconnaissance Group of the Commander-in-Chief of the Luftwaffe) for reconnaissance missions over the Soviet Union. Several Ju 88B-0s were retained by Junkers for developmental testing.

One of these Ju 88B-0s was retro-fitted with improved BMW 801C engines and equipped with an armament of three 13MM MG 131 machine guns; one in the nose, one firing aft from a rear cockpit armored mount, and a third being mounted in a power operated turret installed above the center canopy section. This aircraft (D-ALWN) was designated the Ju 88 V-27, later being re-designated the Ju 88E-0.

The Ju 88 V-27 prototype served as an armament test bed and was later fitted with a forward firing MG 151 20MM cannon. In this form it became one of a series of prototypes that would ultimately lead to the Junkers Ju 188.

Ju 88B-0s of the *Aufklärungsgruppe des Oberbefehlshabers der Luftwaffe* operated on reconnaissance missions over Russia. It is believed that the fuselage band was Yellow, not White as has often been suggested. The Ju 88B-0 had the trailing antenna mast repositioned further back on the fuselage and the FuB1 2 under fuselage antenna was deleted.

Ju 88A-5

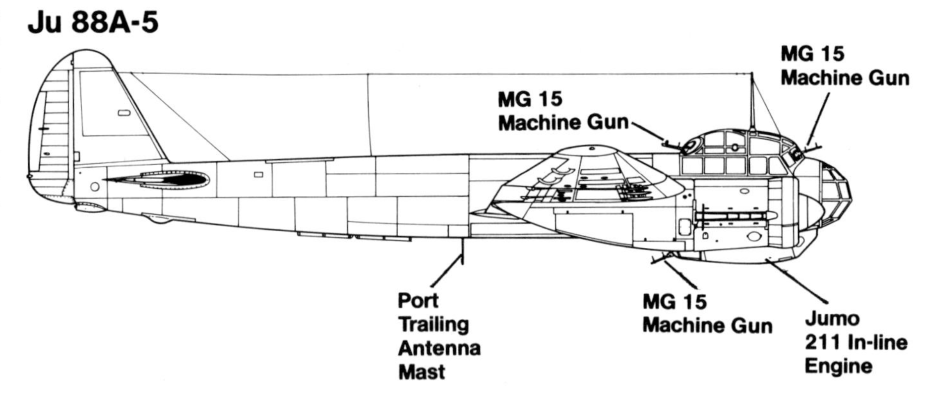

Ju 88B-0

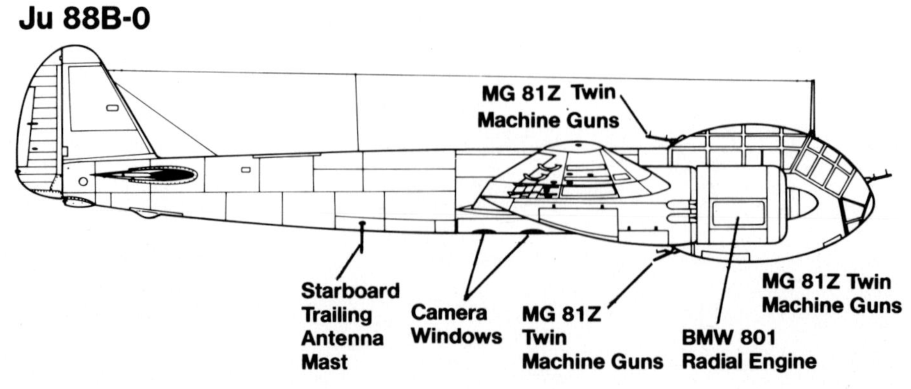

The Ju 88B-3 *Zerstörer* was to have carried a forward firing battery of three 7.92MM MG 17s and a 20MM MG 151 cannon. This armament was first tested on the Ju 88 V-25 prototype, however, the Ju 88B-3 never progressed beyond the original prototype. (USAF via Hunter)

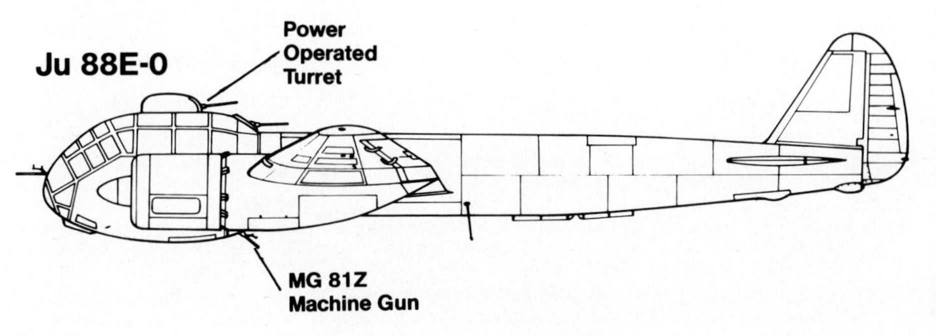

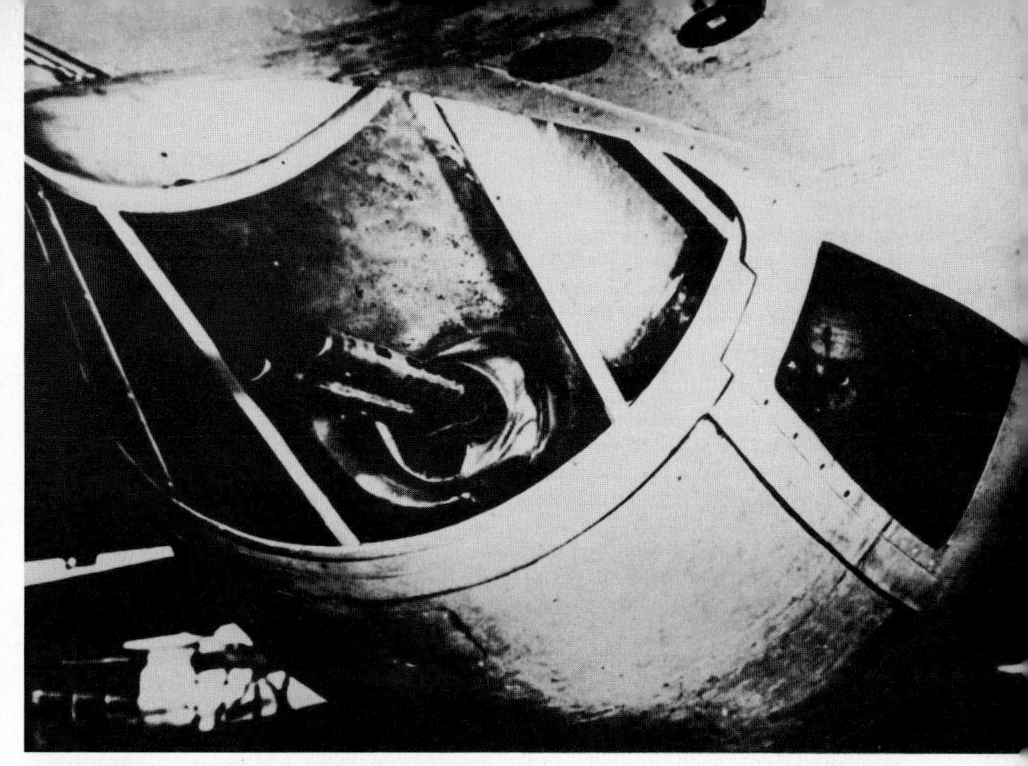

(Above) The smoothly faired ventral gun position on the Ju 88B-0 was armed with an MG 81Z *Zwilling* twin machine gun. (USAF via Hunter)

(Below) The Ju 88 V-27 (D-AWLN) prototype was later redesignated the Ju 88E-0, becoming an armament test-bed for the Ju 188 series. The upper power operated turret and rear canopy gun mount were both equipped with 13MM MG 131 machine guns. The radio antenna mast behind the rear canopy gun was fully retractable. (Gene Stafford)

Ju 88D

Early in the development of the Ju 88 both Junkers and *Luftwaffe* officials began discussions toward development of a long range high speed reconnaissance variant to replace the Dornier Do 17P. By 1940 plans were in motion to produce a dedicated reconnaissance variant of the Ju 88A under the designation Ju 88D. Until production Ju 88Ds became available both the Ju 88A-1 and A-5 were modified for the reconnaissance role.

A number of Ju 88A-1s and Ju 88A-5s were modified for the reconnaissance mission by removing all bombing gear and installing three cameras on a vertical framework in the rear bomb bay. These converted Ju 88s, designated Ju 88A-1(F) and Ju 88A-5(F), were externally identical to their bomber counterparts except for the absence of ETC bomb racks and dive brakes. The four section aft bomb bay doors were replaced with double doors. Two circular camera windows were installed in the starboard door and one in the port door. A 322 gallon fuel tank was usually mounted in the front bomb-bay. The camera controls and a hand operated nose camera were installed in the bombardier's position. A number Ju 88A-1(F)s and A-5(F)s were employed on surveillance missions over Great Britain during the early Summer of 1940.

During 1940 the first of some 330 production Ju 88D reconnaissance aircraft began leaving the Junkers assembly line, joining the Ju 88A-1(F) and A-5(F) in squadron service. Ultimately, five major variants of the Ju 88D would be produced over the next three years. These variants evolved from Ju 88A-4 and A-5 airframes and incorporated most of the progressive modifications and accessory options which appeared on the standard bomber variants, including drop tanks, heavier armament, and radar equipment.

The photographic equipment carried consisted of Rb 70/30 high altitude cameras, Rb 50/30 high altitude cameras, and Rb 20/30 low altitude cameras, in various combinations depending on the mission. Production of the Ju 88D was phased out in 1944, and while sources differ on the total produced, it is believed that between 1,450 and 1,500 machines were built.

Ju 88Ds performed distinguished service on all fronts, serving not only with the *Luftwaffe* but also with a number of Germany's allies, including Romania and Hungary. *Luftwaffe* units equipped with reconnaissance Ju 88s included *Aufklärungsgruppen* 10, 11, 14, 22, 120, 121, 122, 123, and 124; as well as the *Aufklärungsgruppe des Oberbefehlshabers der Luftwaffe*.

With its wheels chocked, an early photo reconnnaissance Ju 88A-1(F) or A-5(F) of 1.(F)/123 runs up its engines during a routine engine test. The dive brakes have been removed, however the mounting brackets near the wing leading edge have been retained. The unit insignia, a *Knullenkopf* (round headed man holding a spyglass), is carried on the engine cowling. (Smithsonian)

Ju 88D-0 and D-2

By mid-1940, a small batch of pre-production Ju 88D-0s had been built, followed shortly by the first production model, the Ju 88D-2. Both aircraft were based on the Ju 88A-5 airframe, equipped with Jumo 211B-1 (for the D-0), G-1 or H-1 engines with the rear bomb-bay camera installation of the earlier Ju 88A-5(F). The ETC bomb racks were installed to carry external drop tanks. It is believed that the first unit to receive the Ju 88D-0 was 1.(F)/122 stationed at Stavenger, Norway. The first unit to become operational with the Ju 88D-2 was 2.(F)/123 operating from bases in France.

A Ju 88D-2 carries the 'flying goose' insignia of 1.(F)/121 under the cockpit. Three optically flat camera windows are visible in the rear bomb bay. 1.(F)/121 operated a mix of Ju 88 reconnaissance aircraft including the Ju 88D-2, tropicalized Ju 88D-4, Ju 88D-1 and Ju 88D-3 for missions in the Mediterranean and North African theaters.

Ju 88D-1

First introduced in early 1941, the Ju 88D-1 was based on the Ju 88A-4. Unlike the Ju 88D-2, the D-1 had its cameras mounted in the fuselage immediately behind the rear bomb-bay. In operational service, however, only the two starboard cameras were carried, while a prepared rivet pattern on the fuselage underside marked the position for an optional third port side camera window. The FuB 12 antenna was moved aft.

The Ju 88D-1 featured an optional gasoline fired heater in the camera compartment with an exhaust vent in a streamlined fairing on the fuselage spine. The camera compartment was accessible for servicing through the rear bomb-bay. The rear of the camera compartment was seperated from the fuselage by a cloth screen.

The Ju 88D-1 was able to carry the complete range of bombs or auxiliary fuel tanks available to the Ju 88A-4. The Ju 88D-1 quickly became the most widely used Ju 88 reconnaissance-bomber variant.

Ju 88D-3

For desert operations, a tropicalized variant of the Ju 88D-1 was produced under the designation Ju 88D-3. Tropical equipment included internal engine air intake sand filters and desert survival gear for the crew. A number of earlier Ju 88D-1 aircraft were modified at *Luftwaffe* conversion centers under the designation Ju 88D-1/Trop.

Ju 88D-4

The Ju 88D-4 was a tropicalized production variant of the Ju 88D-2. Initially these aircraft were designated Ju 88D-2/Trop, however, the designation was later retroactively changed to Ju 88D-4.

Ju 88D-5

The Ju 88D-5 was the final production variant and was produced in parallel with the Ju 88D-1. The D-5 was a general purpose variant with a three camera installation (identical to the Ju 88D-1), tropical equipment, and either Jumo 211G or Jumo 211J engines driving thin chord VDM metal bladed propellers.

(Above) A Whitewashed Ju 88D-1 (F6+TN) of 5.(F)/122 on a snow covered airfield on the Russian front. The fairing on the upper fuselage spine is the exhaust outlet for the optional gas fired camera compartment heater. The Ju 88D-1 was the reconnaissance counterpart to the Ju 88A-4. This early Ju 88D-1 has an early style rudder.

(Bottom) A Ju 88D-2 of the Hungarian Air Force being serviced on an airfield in Russia. The rear bomb-bay doors are open to allow access to the camera equipment. The Hungarian insignia consisted of a Red, White and Green (top to bottom) striped fin and White and Black cross insignia on the fuselage and wings. The fuselage band is Yellow and the fuselage codes are Black with the '9' and '4' outlined in White.

Bundled against the cold, *Luftwaffe* 'Blackmen' hand crank the inertial starter of a Ju 88D-1 (F6+DN) of 5.(F)/122. To clear the camera compartment, the FuB1 2 antenna was moved back on the fuselage. This Ju 88D-1 is fitted with narrow chord VDM metal propellers instead of the standard VS-11 wooden paddle bladed propellers, like the later Ju 88D-5.

Two ground crewmen relax in the shade of a Ju 88D-3 (tropicalized D-1) on a desert field in North Africa. One of the two starboard camera windows is visible behind the rear bomb-bay doors. To extend the range of the Ju 88D-1 drop tanks could be carried on ETC racks retained under each wing root. A fuel line tube is visible between the sway braces.

Camera Installations

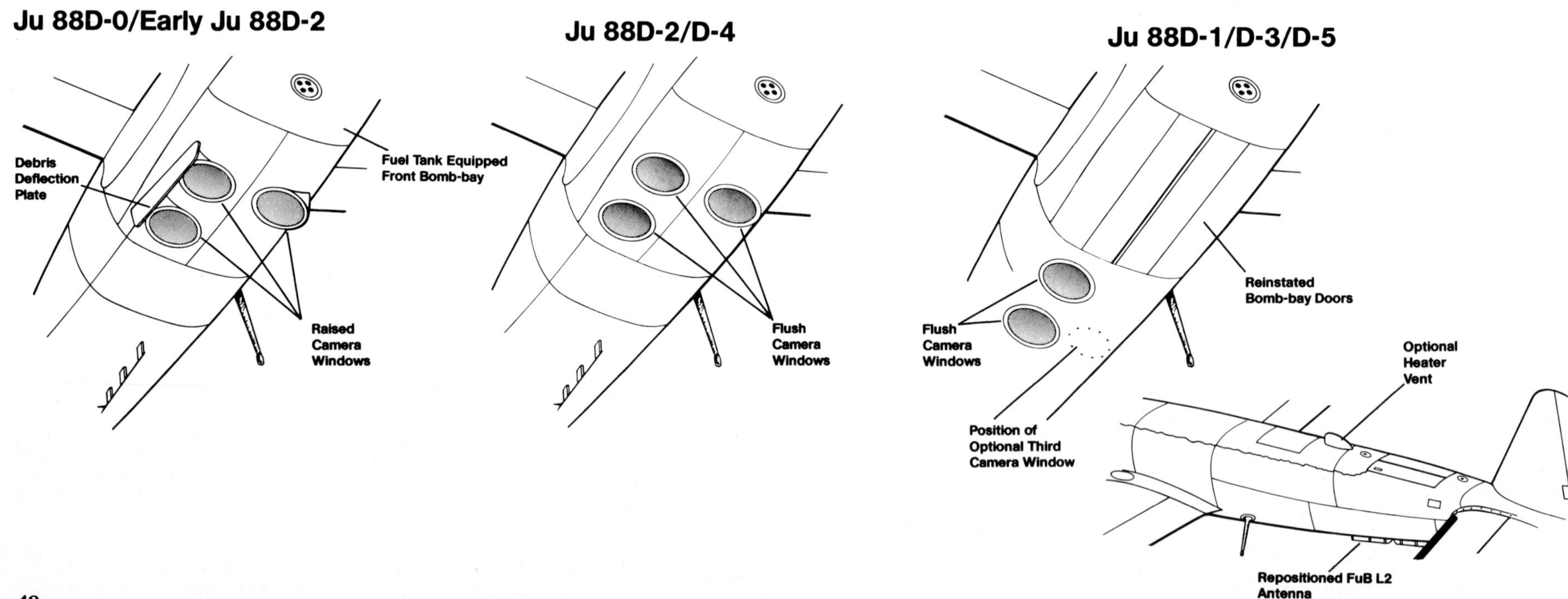

The crew of a Ju 88D-5 of 1.(F)/120 are congratulated after another successful sortie from their Norwegian base. A 20MM MG/FF cannon installation has been fitted to the nose allowing the bomber to attack high priority targets as well as photographing them.

Crewmen of 2.(F)/22 share a light hearted moment on the Russian front while their dark camouflaged Ju 88D-1 warms up its starboard engine. In common with other Ju 88 variants, Ju 88Ds carried a number of different armament configurations — this aircraft carries a single MG 131 in the ventral gun position. The unit insignia of 2.(F)/22 was a Black bear on an 'Ace of Diamonds' playing card.

Aircrews prepare to board a late production Ju 88D-1 (4N+DK) of 2.(F)/22 on a Russian airfield. The under fuselage FuB1 2 rack antenna has been removed and, like many reconnaissance Ju 88s, the windscreen machine gun is not installed. This aircraft has a balanced rudder.

Ju 88H

During late 1942 the RLM issued a request for an ultra-long-range reconnaissance aircraft for missions over the Atlantic. Junker's designers met the requirement with a stretched variant of the Ju 88D under the designation Ju 88H. Developed from a Ju 88D-1 airframe, the Ju 88H had the fuselage stretched 3 feet 3 inches ahead of the wing and 7 feet 6½ inches behind the wing. The ventral gondola was removed to save weight, reducing the crew complement to three. The liquid cooled Jumo engines were replaced with 1,700 hp BMW 801 radial engines housed in shorter more rounded cowlings. A three camera installation was installed in the fuselage, although further back than on the earlier Ju 88D-1. Revised FuG 200 *Hohentwiel* search radar arrays were mounted on the nose, one on either side of the upper nose with a third on the fuselage center line under the nose.

Defensive armament consisted of two 7.9MM MG 81 fixed guns in a WT 81Z weapons pod mounted under the fuselage offset to port, one flexible MG 81 mounted in the rear cockpit, and an optional MG 81 mounted in the starboard windshield.

The fuselage stretch allowed four additional fuel tanks to be mounted in the fuselage (1,242 gallons total) raising fuel capacity with wing tanks and drop tanks to 2,160 gallons total. This fuel load gave the Ju 88H a maximum range of 3,200 miles and gave the bomber the endurance needed for long Atlantic patrol missions.

The first production variant was a radar equipped reconnaissance bomber designated the Ju 88H-1. The Ju 88H-1 was soon followed on the production line by a more heavily armed variant under the designation Ju 88H-2. The Ju 88H-2 was an ultra long range *Zerstörer* variant with the radar and cameras deleted. A solid nose-cap with two MG 151 20MM cannon replaced the bomber nose and four additional MG 151 cannons were carried in a pod mounted under the fuselage offset to port.

Ten examples of the Ju 88H-1 were produced at Merseburg followed by ten Ju 88H-2s. Both aircraft were used in the long range maritime reconnaissance role by the *Fliegerführer Atlantik*.

During 1944 development was begun on progressive developments of the Ju 88H under the designations Ju 88H-3 and Ju 88H-4. These aircraft featured an additional fuselage stretch of 9 feet 9 inches forward of the wing to accommodate a fifth fuselage fuel tank. To improve stability, the vertical tail was enlarged with the fin and rudder being squared off. The BMW 801D engines were replaced by 1,776 hp Jumo 213A-12 liquid cooled inline engines equipped with the MW 50 water-methanol boost.

The Ju 88H-3 was to be a radar-equipped reconnaissance variant, while the Ju 88H-4 was intended to be a *Zerstörer* variant. The deteriorating war situation, however, prevented either type from entering production, the few airframes completed being modified for other projects, such as the *Mistel* flying bomb program.

Ju 88H Development

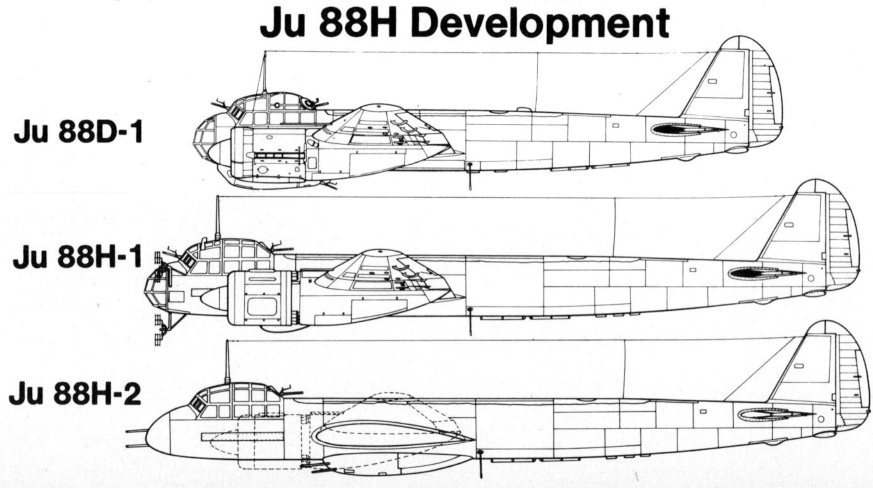

Ju 88S

By late 1942 it had become apparent that the Ju 88A no longer had sufficient performance to evade interception by Allied fighters. As a result, the RLM issued a requirement aimed at improving the performance of the Ju 88A-4, without introducing a radical and time consuming redesign which would interrupt production. Junker's engineers set about modifying a Ju 88A-4 with new engines and other changes under the designation Ju 88S V-1 (originally designated the Ju 88V-93).

While the fuselage, wings, and tail of the Ju 88S V-1 remained unchanged from the Ju 88A-4, the Jumo 211J engines were replaced with 1,700 hp BMW 801D radial engines driving VDM metal propellers. In an effort to reduce drag and weight, the angular 'beetle's eye' nose was replaced by a smoothly rounded transparent nose cap, which was identical in contour to the solid nose caps fitted to Ju 88 fighter variants. To further eliminate drag and reduce weight the ETC bomb racks, dive brakes, and automatic pull-out equipment were deleted, and armor protection was reduced throughout the entire airframe. Bomb-load was restricted to the fuselage bays only.

Defensive armament consisted of an MG 81 mounted in the starboard windscreen, a single 13MM MG 131 in the rear cockpit, and an MG 81Z *Zwilling* twin machine gun in the ventral gondola. Although performance was increased, with maximum speed being raised to 332 mph, the RLM continued to insist on greater improvements in performance. While work was begun to meet the RLM's demands, a limited pre-production run of Ju 88S V1 aircraft were authorized under the designation Ju 88S-0.

Ju 88S-1

To comply with the RLM's demands for increased peformance, the Ju 88S airframe was stripped even more. The ventral gondola was deleted, reducing the crew to three. The bombsight periscope was housed in a small fairing under the starboard nose, similar to that developed for the earlier Ju 88A-15. All but the most vital cockpit armor was removed, and defensive armament was reduced to a single MG 131 with 250 rounds of ammunition in the rear cockpit. A 318 gallon fuel tank was again optional in the forward bomb-bay and ETC 1000 bomb racks, each capable of holding a 2,205 pound bomb load, were mounted under each wing root.

The BMW 801D engines of the Ju 88S-0 were replaced with BMW 801G-2 engines equipped with GM-1 nitrous-oxide boost. The GM-1 installation consisted of three tanks holding 900 pounds of nitrous-oxide with compressed air (which increased combustion and raised engine power 20 per cent) carried in the rear bomb bay. The system allowed two injection rates; a normal rate of 7.95 pounds per engine/per minute for forty-five minutes, or an 'emergency' rate of 13.2 pounds per engine/per minute for twenty-seven minutes. Under boost, top seed was raised from 340 mph (unboosted) to 379 mph

Based on the Ju 88A-4 airframe, the Ju 88S-1 was a stripped high performance variant. The streamlined nose blister, armament and armor reduction, and 1,700 hp BMW 801G radial engines made the Ju 88S-1 the fastest of the Ju 88 bomber series.

(boosted). A maximum altitude of 38,000 feet could be reached with the GM-1 boost, however, service ceiling was normally rated at 34,000 feet. Satisfied with Junker's efforts, the RLM authorized production under the designation Ju 88S-1.

Entering production during late 1943, the Ju 88S-1 became the most numerous and operationally successful of the Ju 88S series. One of the first units to receive the Ju 88S-1 was I/KG 66 which used them alongside Ju 188's in the pathfinder role on the Western Front. During OPERATION STEINBOCK (a series of night raids over England) I/KG66 employed the Ju 88S equipped with receivers for the *Y-Gerät* (Y-Device) system of intersecting directional radio beams to pin-point their targets.

Radio equipment included the FuG 217 *Neptun* which had four vertical antennas mounted under the outer wing panels, FuG 25 IFF transceiver, FuG 101 radio altimeter, and the FuG 16ZY Direction Finder which utilized a small loop antenna carried under the mid-fuselage. The under fuselage FuBl 2 rack antenna was usually not carried on the Ju 88S-1.

Ju 88S-2

A modified variant of the Ju 88S-1 was placed in limited production during the spring of 1944 under the designation Ju 88S-2. The Ju 88S-2 featured the same enlarged under fuselage wooden bomb-bay as the Ju 88A-15, raising maximum bomb load to 6,614 pounds. The ETC bomb racks and GM-1 boost system were deleted with extra fuel tanks installed in the fuselage. The BMW 801D engines were replaced with 1,810 hp BMW 801TJ engines equipped with exhaust driven turbo-superchargers in place of the GM-1 boost system. Defensive armament could be augmented by two fixed rear firing MG 81s in the rear of the wooden bomb-bay.

Ju 88S-3

The Ju 88S-3 represented the last production Ju 88 bomber variant and was manufactured in limited numbers because production emphasis had shifted to Nightfighter production.

The Ju 88S-3 differed from the Ju 88S-1 in that the BMW air cooled radial engines were replaced with Jumo 213A twelve cylinder liquid cooled inline engines driving VS 111 paddle bladed wooden propellers. The cowlings enclosing the Jumo 213s featured a turbo-supercharger intake mounted high on the starboard side of the cowling. Equipped with GM-1 nitrous-oxide boost, the Jumo 213A provided up to 1,776 hp (unboosted), 2,125 hp (normal boost rate), or 2,300 hp (emergency boost) augmented by an additional 340 pounds of thrust from the engine's tuned exhausts. Maximum speed with GM-1 boost was 382 mph (at 27,900 feet).

It is believed that a number of Ju 88S-3s were assigned to I/KG 66 and II/KG 200 during the late summer of 1944 and issued to other units when available. However, by the end of 1944 only a few units of the German bomber force survived, the rest having been neutralized by Allied air superiority over the Reich. In the Spring of 1945 the majority of the surviving Ju 88 bombers were consigned to *Luftwaffe* aircraft 'boneyards', grounded by a lack of fuel and heavy losses of experienced aircrews.

Ju 88S Development

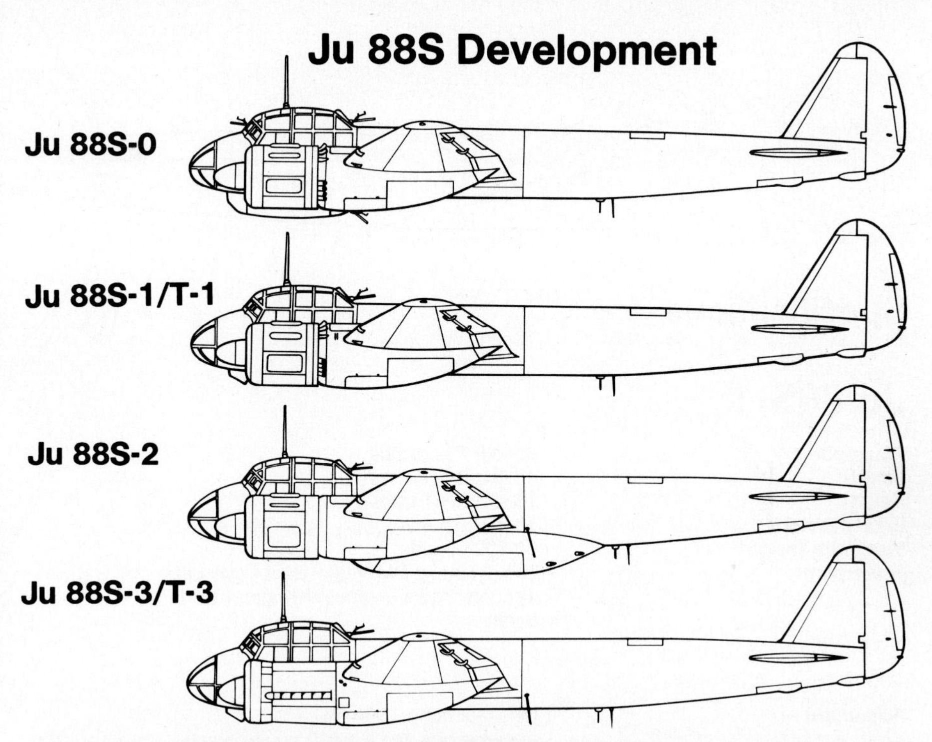

The Ju 88S-3 was a limited production high speed bomber powered by Jumo 213 in-line engines driving VS-111 paddle blade propellers. The Black undersurfaces and mottled night fighter type camouflage (believed to be Light Blue 76 and Gray-Violet 75) indicates that this machine was used in the night pathfinder role.

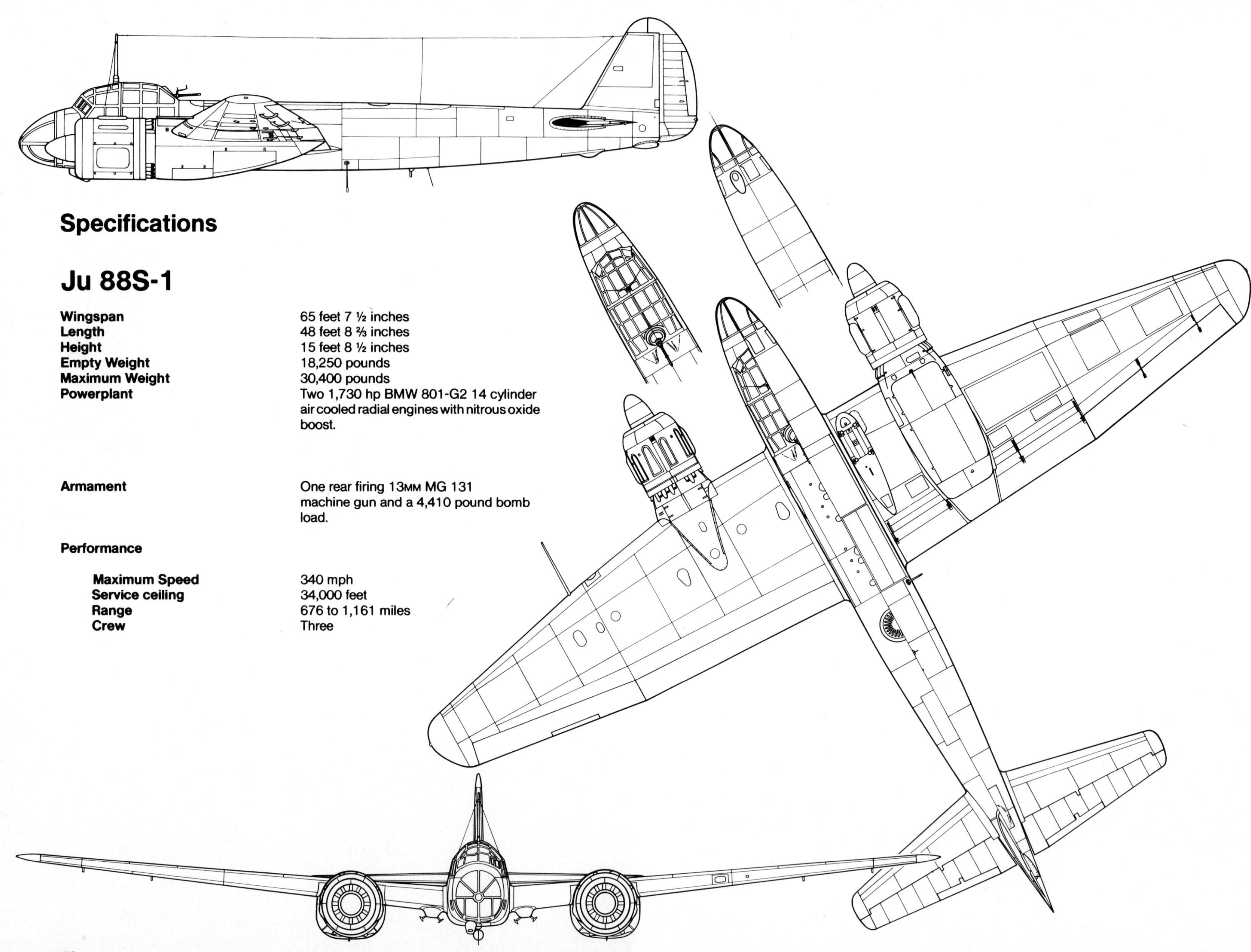

Specifications

Ju 88S-1

Wingspan	65 feet 7 ½ inches
Length	48 feet 8 ⅔ inches
Height	15 feet 8 ½ inches
Empty Weight	18,250 pounds
Maximum Weight	30,400 pounds
Powerplant	Two 1,730 hp BMW 801-G2 14 cylinder air cooled radial engines with nitrous oxide boost.
Armament	One rear firing 13MM MG 131 machine gun and a 4,410 pound bomb load.
Performance	
Maximum Speed	340 mph
Service ceiling	34,000 feet
Range	676 to 1,161 miles
Crew	Three

Ju 88T

With the introduction of the Ju 88S, a reconnaissance variant was developed as a replacement for the Ju 88D. Ultimately only two Ju 88S sub-types, the Ju88S-1 and Ju 88S-3, would be adapted to the photo reconnaissance role under the designations Ju 88T-1 and T-3 with conversion of the Ju 88S-2 variant being considered impractical. The Ju 88T would serve with various *Aufklärungsgruppen*, as well as 1.*Staffel* of the *Versuchverbands* of the *Oberbefehlshabers der Luftwaffe*. Operating alongside Ju 88Ds on both the Eastern and Western fronts and in Italy, Ju 88Ts were in action until the close of the war.

Ju 88T-1

Externally identical to the Ju 88S-1, the Ju 88T-1 had the GM-1 boost system in the rear bomb-bay interchangeable with a 179 gallon fuel tank, while the front bomb-bay carried a 318 gallon fuel tank. The ETC bomb racks were retained to allow the carriage of two 237 gallon drop tanks, although a number of Ju 88T-1s had the ETC bomb racks removed. The bomb sight and its under fuselage housing were removed and the position faired over with sheet metal. The reconnaissance equipment, comprising either two or three Rb 20/30, Rb 50/30, or Rb 70/30 cameras, was installed in the rear fuselage in the same location as on the Ju 88D-1.

The Ju 88T-1 normally carried a crew of three; pilot, radioman/gunner and engineer/camera operator. Defensive armament was generally restricted to a single rear firing MG 131, however, many Ju 88T-1s were field modified with two rear firing MG 81s in the double bulged rear canopy identical to the Ju 88A-4.

Cockpit Development

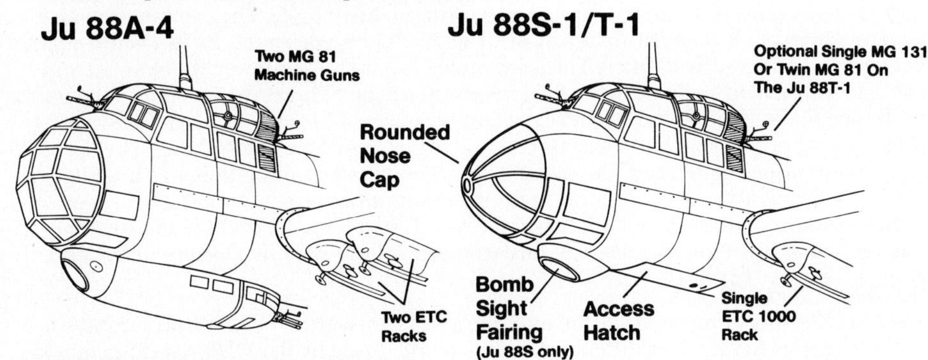

Engine Cowlings

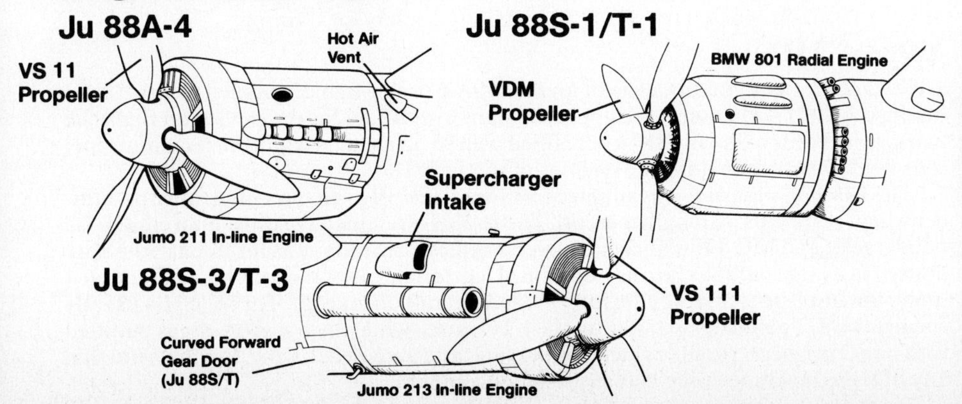

Ju 88T-3

The Ju 88T-3 was a reconnaissance conversion of the Ju 88S-3. Performance of the Ju 88T-3 was similiar to the S-3 except for top speed. Being lighter, the Ju 88T-3 could attain an estimated top speed of 410 mph with the GM-1 boost. The Ju 88T-3 was intended to go into mass production at Henschell/*Schönefeld* during late 1944, however, production was curtailed in favor of increased fighter production after only a few examples had been completed.

A film cartridge is rushed to a waiting courier on a BMW R/75 motorcycle following a reconnaissance mission by *Mizzi*, a Ju 88T-1 (4U+MK) of 2.(F)/123. The fuselage undersurfaces have been painted Black, the propeller spinners are Red, and the name behind the unit insignia is in White.

Mistel Flying Bombs

In one of its final roles the Ju 88 held the promise of being an awesome weapon of tremendous power, but instead it came to represent the type of freakish, 'too-little-too-late' weapons that characterized the final months of the Third Reich. Known variously as the *Vater und Sohn* (Father and Son), *Beethoven Gerät* (Beethoven Device — its official code name), or more commonly the *Mistel* (Mistletoe), this unusual aircraft was composed of two separate components. The lower half was a Ju 88 with a 8,380 pound shaped charge warhead. Mounted above it was a single seat controller fighter on a *Huckepack* (Pick-a-back) superstructure.

The tactics used by *Mistel* units were simple; upon entering a 15 degree dive (approximately ¾ of a mile from a target) the pilot of the fighter (either a Messerschmitt Bf 109 or Focke-Wulf Fw 190) would release the Ju 88 flying bomb and break away. The pilotless Ju 88 would continue on a pre-set course until it crashed into the target, setting off the warhead. The warhead was triggered by a long stand-off probe, sending a one foot diameter stream of molten metal into the target. The shaped charge was capable of penetrating nearly any type of land fortification or armored warship. In tests the warhead successfully penetrated up to sixty feet of reinforced concrete.

The idea for this weapon is generally credited to a Junkers test pilot, Siegfried Holzbauer, who submitted his recommendation to the RLM in 1941. Although such 'composite' aircraft had been flown before, the RLM rejected Holzbauer's concept since there was no conceivable need for such a radical device. By 1943, however, the RLM had revived Holzbauer's proposal and the Ju 88 *Huckepack* project was launched.

The decision to proceed with the project was heavily influenced by a series of successful trials which had been conducted at the *Deutsches Forschungsinstitut für* Segelflug (DFS) during 1942. Light trainers and Bf 109E fighters had been mounted atop DFS 230 troop gliders in a effort to extend the range of the glider. With their considerable experience in this field, the RLM entrusted DFS with the design of the Ju 88's parasite fighter support frame. The final assembly consisted of two steel tube tripods on either wing along with a tail support strut. The main struts ran from the wing spars and center fuselage decking of the Ju 88 to the wing spars of the fighter. The spring loaded tail support strut, when released by the pilot of the fighter, swung downward into a catch yoke on the fuselage spine of the Ju 88. The yoke contained an electrical trigger which fired explosive bolts on the tripod's main attachment points which disconnected the fighter from the support structure.

For striking power, the Ju 88 (initially a Ju 88A-4) was to be fitted with a bulbous six foot diameter warhead attached to the fuselage at the rear cockpit bulkhead. The front half of the warhead was hollow, while the rear half was loaded with 3,800 pounds of explosives (70% hexogen and 30% TNT) and a detonator. The hollow core was coated with a soft metal liner (aluminum or copper) which formed a 'jet' of molten metal during the first micro-second of detonation. Along with the warhead and support frame, the Ju 88 was fitted with a three-axis auto pilot and all unneeded equipment was removed.

The prototype *Mistel* conversion consisted of a standard Ju 88A-4 coupled with a Messerschmitt Bf 109F fighter. Tests of the prototype were successful and in July of 1943 Junkers received instructions to modify fifteen Ju 88A-4 airframes for *Mistel* use under the project code name *Beethoven*. The following *Misteln* were based on Ju 88 bomber and reconnaissance variants.

Mistel S1

The *Mistel* S1 (S for *Schule*, or school) was the primary trainer variant used to train pilots in *Mistel* operations. The lower component was an unarmed Ju 88A-4 with accommodation for a crew of two, while the upper aircraft was a 'stripped' Bf 109F-4. The trainee flew the fighter while a two man instruction crew was carried in the Ju 88. The training crew not only monitored the in-flight separation of the *Mistel* components, but also conducted take off training for the student, since rough takeoffs could easily result in accidents.

Originally intended as a combat version of the *Mistel* 3, the S3A was used solely for training because of the incompatability of the fuels used by the Ju 88A-4 and the FW 190A-6 fighter. On training variants an additional support strut was installed under the nose of the fighter to prevent the propeller from striking the canopy of the Ju 88 on separation. The difference in camouflage schemes between the upper and lower components was not unusual due to the combination of availabile war weary aircraft.

Mistel 1

The *Mistel* 1 was the first combat model, employing a Ju 88A-4/Bf 109F combination. A number of the Bf 109s utilized were reportedly 'hybird' aircraft, a Bf 109F airframe fitted with the more powerful DB 605 engine and cowling of the Bf 109G. The combination was usually ferried to a forward field just prior to a mission where the Ju 88's cabin was detached and the warhead fitted. The use of quick release bolts allowed the change from cabin to warhead to be made in the field in less than a day. Three types of stand-off nose probes could be fitted to the warheads; a conical base probe with an extended shaft; a fully conical probe; or a short flat faced cone for near surface detonations. The tip of these nose probes contained four crush fuses. The *Mistel* combination was unable to achieve a speed in excess of 235 mph, making the aircraft extremely vulnerable to enemy fighters. Adding to the *Mistel's* weight was the use of 50 kg cement bombs in the aft bomb-bay for ballast; mention was made of this arrangement in Allied intelligence documents.

Mistel 3A/S3A

The *Mistel* 3A was a proposed variant utilizing a Ju 88A-4 with an Focke-Wulf Fw 190A-6 as the 'parasite' fighter. The difference in fuel octanes used by the JU 88A-4 (87 octane) and Fw 190A (95 octane) prevented the upper component fighter from utilizing fuel from the tanks of the Ju 88 making the combination unsuitable for combat operations. The *Mistel* 3 was redesignated the *Mistel* S3A and used solely for training.

Mistel 3B

The *Mistel* 3B was a combination of an Fw 190A-6 or A-8 fighter coupled to a stretched fuselage Ju 88H-4 airframe. To supply the fighter with fuel for the outbound flight the fuselage fuel cells of the Ju 88H-4 were filled with 95 octane fuel while the remaining fuel cells held 87 octane fuel for the engines of the Ju 88H-4.

The *Führungsmaschine* was adapted from the *Mistel* 3B as an ultra long range pathfinder which carried its own fighter escort. The Ju 88H-4 retained the three man crew, ETC bomb racks, and MG 131 rear cockpit gun. A centimetric radar was installed in the nose housed in a large bulbous fairing and a third jettisonable landing gear leg was mounted under the fuselage to support the fully loaded aircraft on take off. The Ju 88H-4 usually carried two 237 gallon drop tanks on the ETC racks, while the Fw 190A-8 was outfitted with one *Doppelreiter* (double rider) slipper fuel tank above each wing. It is doubtful that any of these machines were actually used in combat.

***Mistel* Is of IV/KG 101 line an airfield in France armed and ready for a mission. The warheads are fitted with long conical stand-off probes that detonated the warhead at the proper distance from the target. The intended targets of ships and heavy fortifications were gradually abandoned and the probes were shortened to provide a surface blast against targets such as bridges. (M. Hunter)**

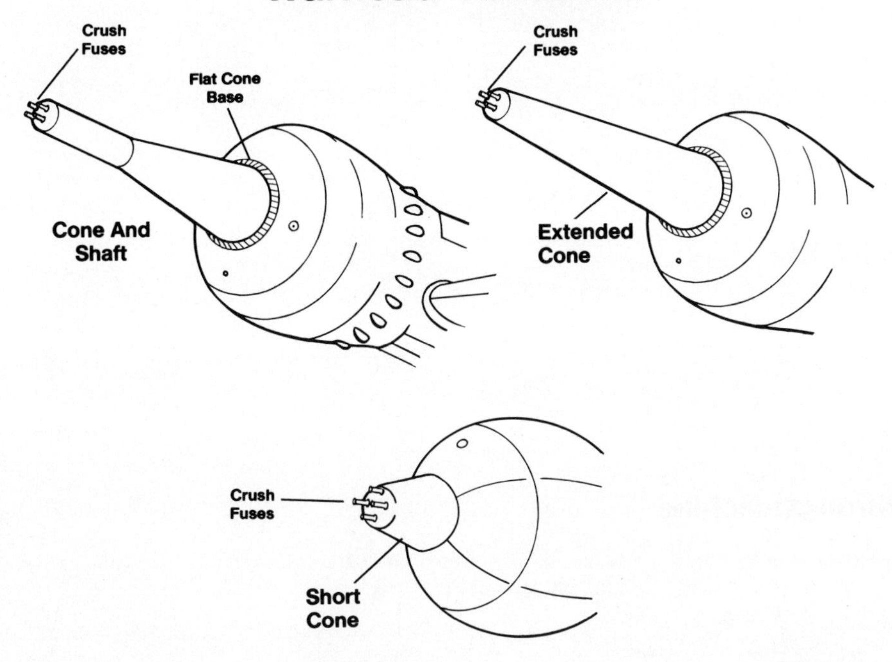

Operations

During the Spring of 1944 pilots of the *Einsatz-Staffel* of IV/KG 101, commanded by *Hauptmann* Horst Rudat, began conversion training on the *Mistel* at Nordhausen. The first planned mission for IV/KG 101 was to be a crippling strike against the British Fleet at Scapa Flow, Scotland. With the Allied invasion of France, however, the unit was quicky shifted to St. Dizier, France. The first operational mission carried out by IV/KG 101 was a night attack against Allied shipping supporting the D-Day beachhead by a single *Mistel* on 24 June 1944. Shortly after this mission the remaining four *Misteln* of IV/KG 101 staged a night attack against Allied shipping in the Seine Bay, escorted by Bf 109G fighters. Although all four of the Ju 88s found their targets, none of the ships attacked were actually sunk.

On 10 October 1944 the *Einsatz-Staffel* of IV/KG 101 was reformed, becoming the nucleus of the *Einsatz-Gruppe* of III/KG 66 which was formed solely for *Mistel* operations. The unit was later redesignated to II/KG 200. While this reorganization was taking place the German High Command developed a plan to use all available *Misteln* for an attack on the British Fleet at Scapa Flow. The aircraft would take off from Grove airfield in Denmark, crossing the North Sea with the navigational assistance of radio marker buoys, accompanied by a *Beleuchter* (Illuminator) *Staffel*. Bad weather continuously delayed the operation until it was finally cancelled.

By the end of 1944 *Mistel* operations were focused on a planned attack against the Soviet armaments industry scheduled for March of 1945 under the code name OPERATION IRON HAMMER. By March of 1945, however, the deteriorating war situation would lead to the abandonment of this plan as well.In the end, most *Mistel* were used in attacks against bridges in an effort to delay the Allied advance. Over 250 Mistels were believed to have been built before the war's end. The number based on Ju 88 bombers is not specifically known.

The *Mistel* 1 utilized a Bf 109F as the upper component and a Ju 88A-4 for the lower component. The appearance of the large warhead leaves little doubt to its destructive power. Fortunately for the Allies, the *Mistel* was 'too little too late', and had no real effect on the war.(M. Hunter)

A Ju 88A-4 lower *Mistel* component was caught by USAAF P-51D Mustangs on 3 February 1945 and shot down. The drag of the fighter support structure and tail support catch yoke on the aft fuselage deck severly restricted the speed and manueverability of the Ju 88 making it an easy kill! (USAF)

Mistel Development

Mistel S1

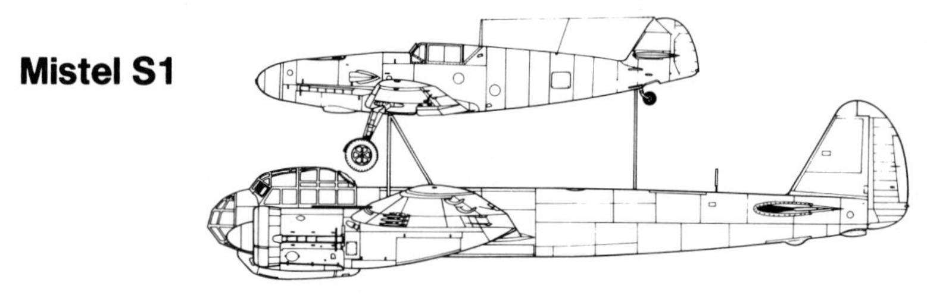

Mistel 1

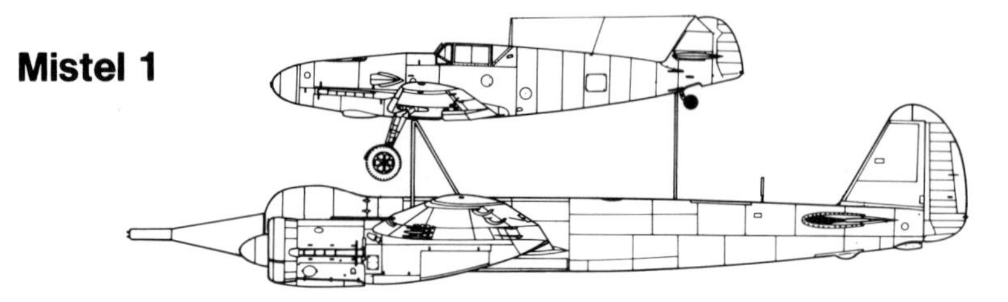

Mistel S3A

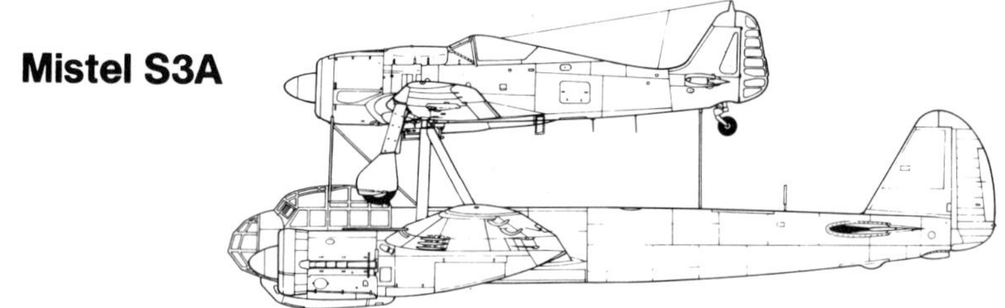

Mistel 3B

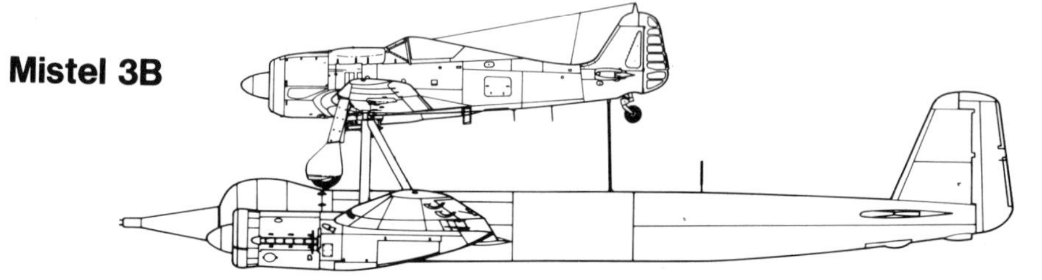

Führungsmachine

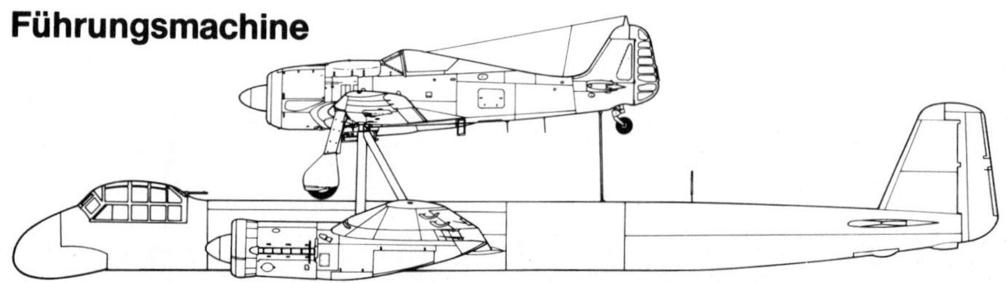

Unusual Variants

In researching the Ju 88 it soon became obvious that the adaptability which made the Ju 88 such a formidable weapon also created its share of non-standard unusual variants. The interchangeability of components led to a number of variants which have yet to be fully documented. The individual 'tinkerings' of *Luftwaffe* personnel in the field resulted in variations of the Ju 88 which frequently defy textbook description.

For example, the Ju 88A-4/U, which is mentioned in Allied intelligence reports, appears to have no outstanding difference to set it apart from a standard Ju 88A-4 except for the installation of *Kuto-Nase* cable cutters in the wing leading edges. The 'U' designation was commonly used to indicate a *Umbau* (rebuilt) status such as the Ju 88A-6/U. It is believed that the Ju 88A-4/U was a designation for early Ju 88A-4 airframes 'recycled' for equipment updating, or for earlier Ju 88 variants which were re-manufactured to Ju 88A-4 standards.

The Ju 88A-4/R designation (which at one time was often mentioned in a number of previously published Ju 88 histories) has been credited with indicating the initial variant equipped with Jumo 211J power plants. It is believed, however, that the designation may have indicated a modification of the basic Ju 88A-4 using a field conversion kit, which would be appropriate for the installation of optional equipment packages such as the 20MM MG/FF cannon installation.

In other instances, photograpic evidence has surfaced showing a number of unique Ju 88 modifications, such as Ju 88D's with the ventral gondolas removed, a Ju 88A-4 with a field installed flame thrower mounted below the tail, and a highly unusual reconnaissance aircraft assigned to 1.(F)/120. This aircraft had Jumo 211J in line engines driving thin-chord propellers (similar to the Ju 88D-5), but had the complete nose section of a Ju 88T-1.

The Ju 88 could assume personalities as unique and individual as the men who flew them. Literally, it seemed that anything was possible with the Ju 88 except, in the end, victory. To quote one famous Ju 88 pilot, Jochen Helbig; "The Ju 88 was a winner . . . in the right hands a top notch plane." A fitting tribute for a remarkable aircraft.

Ju 88 Unknown Variant

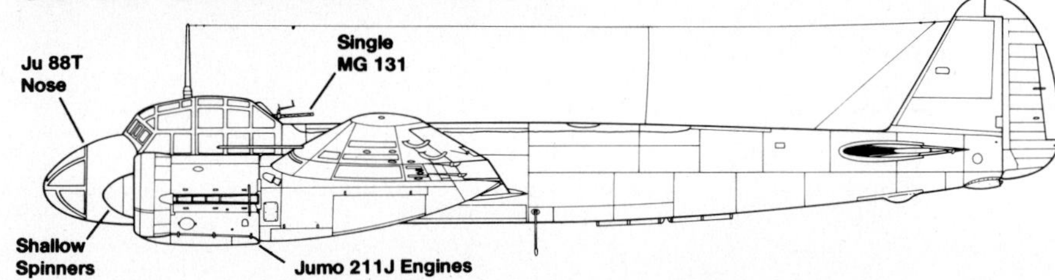

A highly unusual modification was carried by this Ju 88A-4 (9K+FB, Werk-Nr. 1050) of II/KG 51 in Romania during 1941. The bomber was field modified with two flame thrower tubes mounted under the rudder. Although successfully tested, the oil fed flame thrower never reached operational status on the Ju 88.

With its adaptability, the Ju 88 could be molded into variants which defy straight textbook descriptions. This aircraft carries a gondola mounted cannon, FuG 200 radar, sun shades over the gun sights, and flame dampening exhaust shrouds. With this combination of equipment it could be a either a late Ju 88A-4, Ju 88A-14, late Ju 88D-1 or or Ju 88D-3.

Aircraft

Armor

Weapons

Warships

squadron/signal
publications

in action